Investment Management
With Your Personal Computer

Richard C. Dorf

COMPUTE! Publications,Inc.abc
One of the ABC Publishing Companies
Greensboro, North Carolina

Printed in the United States of America

ISBN 0-87455-005-X

10 9 8 7 6 5 4 3 2 1

The opinions expressed in this book are solely those of the author and are not necessarily those of COMPUTE! Publications, Inc.

COMPUTE! Publications, Inc., Post Office Box 5406, Greensboro, NC 27403, (919) 275-9809, is one of the ABC Publishing Companies, and is not associated with any manufacturer of personal computers. Apple, Apple II, and Apple III are registered trademarks, and Macintosh is a trademark of Apple Computer, Inc. Commodore 64 is a trademark of Commodore Electronics Limited. IBM PC, PCjr, PC/XT, and PC/AT are trademarks of International Business Machines, Inc. Tandy 2000 and TRS-80 are trademarks of Tandy, Inc. TI Professional is a trademark of Texas Instruments, Inc.

Contents

Reviewed Products and Services

Chapter 5. Trading Securities by Computer

Chapter 6. Portfolio Management

Chapter 7. Fundamental Analysis

Chapter 8. Technical Analysis

Chapter 9. Investment Simulations and Games

Chapter 10. Statistics and Graphics

Chapter 11. Bonds and Mutual Funds

Chapter 12. Futures and Options Contracts

Chapter 13. Tax and Financial Planning

Foreword

Investing is a challenge. Not only do you have to make decisions about what to buy and sell, but you have to know when. Add to that the volumes of figures which have to be tracked, even in a moderately-sized portfolio. Fortunately, personal computers—relative newcomers to investment management—can help tremendously as you try to second-guess the market. Computers can help you assess your portfolio, access enormous electronic databases brimming with economic and corporate information, and chart the ups and downs of almost any market. There's only one catch—you need the right software.

Software is what makes your personal computer do what you want it to do. Without software (programs), your computer is only so much silicon and steel. Choosing the right software, or even the right database, can be just as hard as figuring out the market. There are hundreds of programs, dozens of databases, to pick from.

Investment Management with Your Personal Computer gives you all the necessary information to make an intelligent choice. Over 130 software packages, databases, and investment services are listed and reviewed in this book. You'll discover what each does, or doesn't do. You'll find ways to make managing your investments easier, more efficient, and thus more profitable; why one program is better than another; and how much each costs.

Written by an investor who uses a personal computer, *Investment Management with Your Personal Computer* includes evaluations of spreadsheets, telecommunication packages, portfolio managers, fundamental and technical analysis tools, investment simulations, statistics and graphics software, bond and mutual funds aids, futures and options contract manipulators, and tax and financial planning programs. Prices and manufacturers are listed, and well-written summaries tell you what you can expect from the program.

You'll also find reviews of numerous electronic databases. They range from the well-known to the unknown, and can provide almost any information you need to make your investment decisions count. There are even listings of brokerage houses which offer online trading, letting you place orders when *you* want, from the comfort of your own home or office.

All this information makes it easier to decide what software and services you need. You'll be able to make more intelligent buying decisions.

You probably already know how to manage your investments. But with a personal computer, the right software, the best information database, and your broker, you'll quickly discover that you can be an even better investor.

Dedication

It is my pleasure to thank my research assistant, Andrew Fagan, now a professional investment manager, and my secretary, Laura J. Gholson, who performed superbly. I wish to dedicate this book to my daughter Christine, who enjoys discussing these markets with me.

R.D.
Davis, California
March 1985

Personal Computers

Personal Computers

A Brief Introduction

The word *computer* brings up all kinds of images. Vast rows of metal-cased cabinets, blinking lights, and tapes spinning at high speed—or the portable that fits inside a briefcase. Both are computers. Both are simply devices able to accept information (*input*), process that information, and provide some sort of results of that processing (*output*).

There's been considerable discussion in the past decade of the information explosion—the exponential growth of knowledge at a rate that's overwhelming us. There *is* hope, however, that computers and information processing will provide a new framework for information and will increase our ability to synthesize and integrate information.

We're usually looking for two things in a computer: increased speed and increased quality of processing. Accounting is a good example of something most readily accomplished by a digital computer system. Over the years, the accounting process has shifted in large part from ledgers to punched cards, then to computer processes.

But what makes up a computer? It's not just a box on a desk or in an air-conditioned room. It has several distinct parts, all of which must be present in order to process this mass of information we're often faced with. In fact, five basic parts, when combined, create a computer.

- An **input unit** or function, which accepts the necessary input data and instructions.
- A **storage** or **memory unit,** in which the computer instructions, the data, and the intermediate results are stored.
- An **arithmetic unit,** in which numbers can be added, subtracted, compared in size with other numbers, and so on.
- An **output unit,** which provides the desired results in suitable form, such as a printed number.
- A **control unit,** which controls the other four units, directs their order of operation, and supervises the overall operation of the computer.

Figure 1-1. Parts

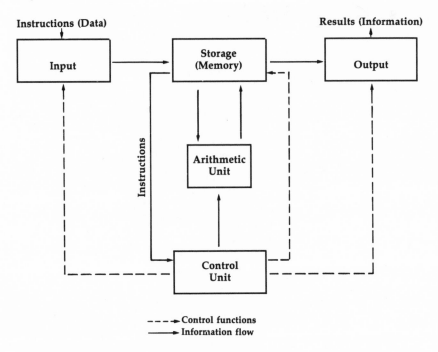

The arithmetic and control functions are accomplished by the central processing unit, or CPU. But the basic unit of the electronic digital computer is the arithmetic unit. It performs the arithmetic operations accurately, reliably, and at high speed. Its high speed would be wasted, however, if during each operation it had to go back to the input unit for the same information at every step. Instead, the storage unit holds the data, the instructions, and the intermediate results of the calculation.

Since the instructions are stored in memory, as are the intermediate results, it's possible for the computer to modify the instructions themselves as the calculation progresses.

The control unit supervises the flow of information and calculations and requests from memory the instructions and data necessary at each stage in the calculation sequence. (The control functions are shown as dotted lines in figure 1-1.)

The input and output units serve as connections between you and the machine. A keyboard is a good example of an input device. Data may be stored on a disk storage device for later access. The process of transferring information from such a device into the main storage unit and then to the user is known as an output operation.

The Advent of Personal Computers

Small, inexpensive desktop computer systems have been available since 1975. They provide significant computing power, but at relatively slower speeds when compared with larger computers. These small computers are often called *micro-computers*, since the computer is based on a *microprocessor* constructed from integrated circuit devices, or chips. The microprocessor carries out the functions of the central processing unit of a computer; it consists of the arithmetic unit and the control unit. When a main memory and input/output system are added to the microprocessor, the entire system becomes a microcomputer.

A typical microcomputer contains a relatively small main memory, weighes about 25 pounds, consumes 30 watts of power, and costs less than $10,000. Microcomputers, in contrast to *minicomputers*, trade power for price and size. More often, you'll hear microcomputers termed *personal computers*, because they can be bought and used by just one person or shared by several people. Today, the term *personal computer* generally refers to a computer system that fits on a table or desktop, has a consumer product price range, and is marketed for a wide range of personal applications.

Nowadays, it's almost impossible to categorize a personal computer by its memory size or computing power, simply because these things are changing so rapidly. What was once a powerful machine, perhaps one with 64K (kilobytes) of memory, may be too weak for today's more sophisticated applications.

Hardware

The physical equipment of a computer is called *hardware*. It, too, comes in several distinct parts. Take a look at figure 1-2, which shows an Apple IIe computer—the hardware.

Figure 1-2. Apple IIe

The Apple IIe computer with Apple monitor and one floppy disk drive. Courtesy of Apple Computer, Inc.

In the **Apple IIe**, the *system unit*, the heart of a personal computer, houses the microprocessor, read only memory (ROM), random access memory (RAM), power supply, and eight expansion slots, which can be used to attach options. One or two 5-1/4-inch disk drives can be connected to the system unit.

A *monochrome display*, as shown in figure 1-2, is a high-resolution green or amber display. This particular monitor features an 11-1/2-inch screen with an antiglare surface and a variety of highlighting choices. Most screens display 25 lines of 80 characters each, though some computers (like the IIe) can show only 40-character-wide lines. (The IIe is capable of displaying 80 columns only when an additional board is placed in the computer.) Most displays support 256 different letters, numbers, and special characters.

In the IIe's case, the *keyboard* is connected to the system unit. Other computers have a detachable keyboard. The IIe features 63 keys and offers commonly used data and word processing functions in a design that resembles the familiar typewriter layout.

Data and instructions may be stored on a *floppy disk* for use at a later time. A floppy disk is a thin, flexible Mylar disk coated with a magnetic film; it's permanently enclosed in a slotted jacket. The jacket protects the disk as it rotates within the jacket, and the slot functions as a window for the disk drive's read/write head.

Figure 1-3. The Floppy

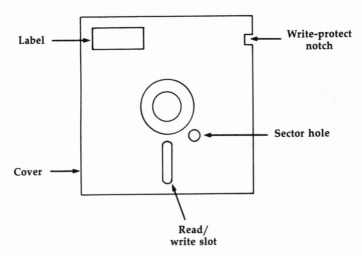

A personal computer uses *read only memory (ROM)* to store startup programs. ROM is simply memory space into which information is placed at the time of manufacture. Such information is available at any time and remains unchanged. Normally, it cannot be modified. The contents of ROM, which remain when power is removed, are often called *firmware*, which is simply software programs embedded in hardware.

A *hard, fixed disk drive* is a possible add-on to a personal computer. The fixed disk is a flat metal object coated with magnetic material that stores information. It's capable of storing up to a hundred times more information than a floppy disk. Hard-disk drives are most often sealed units containing one or more disks that you cannot remove. For the most part, they're valuable only when you have mass amounts of data which you want to retrieve quickly.

A personal computer is capable of producing written copy, often called *hardcopy*, by using a printer. Many manufacturers offer a dot-matrix printer, in which the characters are formed from multiple dots. Many dot-matrix printers are capable of printing over 80 characters per second. If you require printed output in a quality similar to that of a typewriter, you'll need a letter-quality printer.

The letter-quality printer provides a fully formed character. Typical letter-quality printers use a daisywheel, which is a printing element shaped in the form of a disk. Each character is located at the end of a "petal" connected at the hub of the disk. Behind the spinning wheel is a small hammer, controlled by the computer's signals. Daisywheel printers usually operate in the range of 20 to 55 characters per second.

Keep in mind that dot-matrix printers are normally less expensive than letter-quality printers, though that distinction is tending to blur. Some daisywheel printers, for example, can be purchased for as little as $400.

Put all these (or at least most of them) together, and you have a personal computer system. A typical system is listed below. Of course, yours may be quite different.

Unit	Specifications
Main memory	16K read-only memory; 64K or 128K random-access memory
Disk storage	Two floppy disk drives, using 5-1/2-inch single-sided or double-sided disks capable of storing 160K or 320K each
Keyboard	63 full-function keys, including 10 for numeric entry and cursor control
Monochrome display	24 lines of 80 characters each on an 11-1/2-inch screen; uppercase and lowercase letters
Dot-matrix printer	80 characters per second printed

Choosing the Computer

Unfortunately, you aren't really able to choose a computer for use with investment software from all the possible machines. In fact, you'll be limited to the kind of computers which run the software you need. Most of the readily available investment software has been developed for the IBM PC series (PC,

PC/XT, and sometimes the PCjr), IBM PC-compatible computers, or for the Apple II series. In the near future, many investment programs may be available for Apple's Macintosh
computer. If you simply want to access a database and use
your own spreadsheet analysis (on paper or through the computer), then your choice will be wider and could even include
such lap-portable computers as the Radio Shack 100.

Prices for a complete computer system vary widely.
Depending on your needs (do you need a printer or a modem?) and the software you want, you can put together a system for anywhere from $2,000 to $10,000. You can begin with
a computer with 64K of RAM and add memory as appropriate.
You can also later add a wider range of printers, disk drives,
and other peripheral devices. You don't have to buy everything at once.

As you consider a specific computer for your investment
purposes, you should keep several things in mind. What will
be the nature and volume of the work you'll do? Can the computer be expanded? What kind of service is available?

The applications you want your computer to handle are
also of vital importance. If you want to be able to prepare your
investment tax reports, for instance, and there's no such software available for your computer, you'll have to do without it.
Take a look at the list below—many of the applications for
investment management are included. Decide which you want
your computer to be able to do for you, and make sure the
computer you choose has software to fit those needs.

• Accounting and financial management
• Word processing for reports
• Computer-assisted investment analysis
• Inventory of personal investments
• Personal finance
• Investment tracking
• Tax preparation
• Maintaining schedules and mailing lists of potential
  investments
• Communicating with remote databases or other personal
  computers
• Storing data on selected investments
• Generating graphs and charts

Once you've decided on the applications you want to emphasize, you should review and select the programs that meet your objectives and then purchase, rent, or lease a personal computer.

If at all possible, try to select the software first. You don't need to buy it, just choose which program(s) you're sure you'll want. Only then should you start looking for a computer to run that software. If you must choose a computer first, you should pick one that will support a wide range of software, and that has good data communications and data storage facilities. Both of these are important if you're planning to access large databases of investment information and use that data to make investment decisions.

Some of Your Choices

The first Apple II was introduced in early 1977. Since then, it has evolved into several versions. The Apple II+ is no longer available, although thousands of them are still in use. Today, you can buy an Apple IIe or Apple IIc computer system. Each can be used, as is, in business or at home.

The Apple IIe has already been described and illustrated. The **Apple IIc**, however, is relatively new. Introduced in April 1984, this portable version of the Apple II series weighs only 7-1/2 pounds. Like the IIe, it requires a monitor or television set. The Apple IIc 9-inch monitor displays 24 lines and 80 columns. A 24-line, 80-column liquid crystal display (LCD), which weighs less than 3 pounds, is also available from Apple.

Although it measures only 2-1/2 × 12 × 11-1/2 inches, the IIc includes an internal 5-1/4-inch 140K disk drive. It can also accommodate a mouse similar to that used by the Macintosh.

The IIc includes a standard 128K of RAM. It uses a low-power version of the Apple II 6502 microprocessor and can run 90 percent of the Apple II series software. The computer can be connected to a variety of peripheral devices, from a second disk drive or joystick to a modem or printer. External batteries for powering the LCD screen are available from third-party manufacturers.

The IIc includes a 63-key, full-travel keyboard. Both uppercase and lowercase are supported. A total of 128 characters can be displayed. There's also a conveniently located Reset button, a 40/80 column switch for a television set or video monitor, a power-on light, and a light that indicates when the disk drive is active.

You should be able to put together a basic dual-disk drive IIc system, with display and printer, for approximately $2,000.

Figure 1-4. The Apple IIc

The Apple IIc is a miniaturized and enhanced version of the Apple IIe. It is transportable and includes 128K of RAM and a half-height disk drive in a 7-1/2-pound unit. The Apple monitor is designed to complement the IIc. Courtesy of Apple Computer, Inc.

In January 1984, Apple announced its newest computer, the **Macintosh**. Although investment software has been slow to appear, the computer's popularity and the fact that it's currently aimed at the business market should insure additional software.

The Macintosh is a different kind of computer. In many places, the designers have substituted symbols, called *icons*, for menus and for commands that must be typed in on other computers. They've simplified keyboard activity, replacing most function and special-purpose keys with a pointing device called a *mouse*. And the machine's operating system invites all Macintosh programmers to integrate the mouse and icons into their programs' command structures.

The mouse is a small hand-held unit. Rolling it about on the tabletop next to the computer moves a cursor on the screen. You move the mouse to position the cursor on an icon and click a button on the mouse. That executes the chosen activity.

Figure 1-5. The Macintosh

The Macintosh with mouse and detachable keyboard. Peripheral devices such as a numeric keypad, external 3-1/2-inch drive, Imagewriter printer, modem, and carrying case are also shown. Courtesy of Apple Computer, Inc.

The **IBM Personal Computer (PC)** was introduced in August 1981. Primarily a business computer, many have found their way into homes. The typical PC has 128K or more of memory, with two disk drives capable of storing 320K on a double-sided disk. The IBM monitor displays 25 lines of 80 characters each. It supports 256 different letters, numbers, and characters which are formed in a 9 X 14 dot matrix. A typical IBM PC system, including monitor and dot-matrix printer, costs from $3,000 to $4,000.

IBM also sells two advanced versions of the PC: the PC/XT and the PC AT. These machines provide additional enhancements for the more advanced and demanding user. In addition, IBM still supports the now-discontinued PCjr, a 128K, single-disk drive computer which can run some PC software.

There are many companies selling computers which perform similarly to the IBM PC and utilize the PC's operating system. These IBM PC compatibles are often called *PC clones*.

Figure 1-6. The IBM PC

The IBM Personal Computer with two disk drives and a printer. Courtesy of International Business Machines, Inc.

Hardware Isn't Everything

Of course, a computer is virtually useless unless it has something to do. And it won't do much for you unless it's running *software*, the programs you've chosen. The remainder of this book details investment management software, explicitly describing just what's out there and available in a number of investment areas. What you choose to buy will be up to you, of course, and will depend on your needs and pocketbook.

This guide gives you the chance to make informed buying decisions. With it, you can explore the wide variety of financial and analytical programs which can make you a more productive (and profitable) investor. Having the right software is critical to turning your computer into the most powerful investment management tool imaginable.

Computer-Aided Investing

Computer-Aided Investing

Investments

An *investment* is any vehicle into which funds can be placed with the expectation that they will be preserved, or increase in value and generate positive returns.

Idle cash is not an investment, since its value is likely to be eroded by inflation and it fails to provide any type of return. The same cash placed in a bank savings account *is* an investment, since the account provides a positive return (the interest the bank pays you). Investments can be categorized by a number of factors, such as whether the investment is a security or property; direct or indirect; debt, equity, or option; low or high risk; and short or long term.

Investments that represent evidence of debt, ownership of a business, or the legal right to acquire or sell an ownership interest in a business or in property are called *securities*. The most common types of securities are bonds, stocks, and options.

Many people make investments in *real property* or *tangible personal property*. Real property is land, buildings, anything permanently fixed to the land. Tangible personal property includes things like gold, antiques, and art.

Although security investments are more common among individual investors, many people prefer property investments because they feel more comfortable owning something they can see and touch. But because there's an organized mechanism for buying and selling securities, and because of their widespread popularity, we'll focus on securities, not property investments.

Generally, investment is distinguished from *speculation* by both time and the risk/return characteristics. The true investor is interested in a good rate of return, earned on a rather consistent rate for a relatively long period of time. On the other hand, the speculator seeks opportunities promising very large returns, earned rather quickly. Obviously, this makes the speculator less interested in consistent performance than the investor.

The speculator is more interested in an abnormal, extremely high rate of return than the normal, moderate rate. And a speculator wants to get these high returns in a short time.

Figure 2-1. Speculation?

"You could make a fast buck on this one, if you don't mind holding it for a couple of years."

Courtesy of Sidney Harris

Not all investments have the same returns for a given period. Table 2-1 shows the value of $10,000 invested over the three year period from June 30, 1981 to June 30, 1984. Notice the difference in just two of the investment possibilities, New York Stock Exchange stocks (represented by the NYSE index), and Ginnie Mae bonds. If an investor purchased a portfolio of the former, he or she would have achieved only a 16 percent return. Ginnie Mae bonds, on the other hand, would have returned 55 percent. A big difference.

Table 2-1. Value of $10,000 Investment

Rank	Item	Value after 3 years
1.	Ginnie Mae Bonds	$15,501
2.	Corporate Bonds	15,398
3.	Yankee Bonds	15,207
4.	Treasury Bonds	14,562
5.	Income Funds	14,277
6.	Money Market Funds	13,855
7.	Municipal Bond Funds	13,702
8.	Growth Funds	12,644
9.	Old Masters Paintings	12,311
10.	Passbook Account	11,816
11.	NYSE Stocks	11,606
12.	Common Stocks	11,145
13.	OTC Stocks	11,107
14.	Coins	10,971
15.	Single Family Home	10,960
16.	AMEX Stocks	10,681
17.	Chinese Ceramics	10,000
18.	Silver	9,907
19.	Gold	9,147

Source: Fact, Sept. 1984, pp. 11

The actual investment return is expressed as the ratio obtained by dividing the income, plus capital gain or loss, by the total investment. Thus, to calculate the return of the NYSE stock portfolio, just divide the income ($1,106) by the investment ($10,000), for a result of 16 percent.

Risk is the possible loss of income or capital or the unavailability or variability of expected return. It's assumed that investors attempt to maximize wealth, something accomplished by maximizing return and minimizing risk. This might be done by protecting capital, by increasing income or capital, and by reducing risk.

A majority of working Americans have investments directly—in stock, real estate, bonds—or indirectly—through their pension or mutual funds. There are some 35 million stockholders in the United States; the average portfolio is about $12,000. In other words, more people are investors, or likely to become investors, than one might think.

Investment Methods

There are three investment approaches commonly adopted by investors:

- The fundamental approach
- The technical approach
- The modern portfolio theory approach

The *fundamental* approach assumes that rigorous analysis of each company will result in selecting stocks that are undervalued. The investor would select stocks based on an economic analysis, an industry analysis, and a company analysis. The stocks are held as long as they promise a high return. They're sold if the investor thinks they've become overpriced. Chances are they'd be held for relatively long periods of time. Some fundamental investors follow a buy and hold policy by selecting quality stocks and holding them for a long period. The fundamental approach is followed by the majority of financial institutions.

The *technical* approach to investment emphasizes that the behavior of the price of the stock and perhaps the volume of trading will determine the stock's future price. This method centers on plotting the price movement of the stock and drawing inferences from that movement. The technical investor then selects a few stocks for purchase and trades in these issues. The emphasis is on capital gains or price appreciation in the short run.

Modern portfolio theory assumes that the market is efficient and that information is widely available about the market and individual stocks. New information is quickly transferred to the marketplace, and a new price is established. Since the marketplace is efficient, stock prices of one moment are independent from prices in the next moment. The theory states that it's impossible to predict future prices. Information is known to all, and no one, on average, can do much better than the market. In addition, securities with the same risk level tend to provide similar return.

Investors using this theory assume that they can't beat the market. So they diversify to have enough securities to provide them with the average return of the market. Since they cannot predict, they follow a buy-and-hold philosophy. Their attitude toward risk is determined by the amounts invested in riskless *and* risk securities, which is comparable to the return of the market as measured by some market index. Modern security analysis emphasizes risk and return estimates while the more traditional fundamental analysis emphasizes the calculation of an intrinsic value of a stock or set of stocks.

Using a Computer for Investing

Most of the techniques of investment analysis can be done with a desk calculator, but that's really only feasible for a limited number of securities. More important, it takes a huge amount of time. The computer can assist in the calculations, the storage of information, and the ability to change underlying assumptions in projections. All these abilities make the computer a perfect tool for investors.

Most investors buy an applications program designed specifically for the analytical approach they want to emphasize. There are two basic types of programs: analytical and portfolio management. The analysis may be a fundamental or technical analysis. The portfolio management system helps you to manage your investment holdings by keeping track of your past actions and of any gains or losses.

Of course, a program cannot replace sound judgment and the calculations are only as good as the information given it, and the forecasts or assumptions you provide.

What a computer can do best is make vast and complicated calculations quickly, organize and reorganize data efficiently for reporting and analyzing, and, when connected to a database, provide a variety of past and current economic and financial news and information that can be used for making investment decisions. To best take advantage of all that, and to justify the often considerable cost, you should at least be a moderately active trader interested in improving your investment performance.

Investment analysis is a multistep process that results in selecting investments most suitable for you. The steps include:

- Defining your investment objectives
- Determining the type of investments meeting your objectives
- Determining the cost, risk, and potential returns for each possible investment
- Selecting one or more investments
- Managing the investments

The application programs you select will help you the most with the third, fourth, and fifth steps. Before buying any applications software, then, be sure you've completed the first and second steps yourself. The computer and its software are only tools. You must carefully determine your objectives and obtain accurate, high quality data and make reasonable forecasts of economic variables.

With investment software, you can learn to make better investments, manage your portfolio, and prepare year-end tax reports faster and more accurately.

Advantages of Computer-Aided Investing

You can use a computer to meet many of the challenges you'll face as an individual investor. You can engage in personal financial planning and management; profit planning; market assessment and timing; and stock, bond, and commodities trading using the computer. Through your computer you can keep track of your various accounts *and* coordinate all your investments. Computers assist in the recording and retrieval of the data on your investments. Some computer programs even help you spot major trends and important changes in the market.

The tracking and evaluation of any type of investment is a mathematical operation. Not surprisingly, the more volatile investments, like commodities and options, require more complex mathematical tools to discern patterns in price movements.

Since a computer is basically a mathematical tool for solving complex problems quickly, and since uncertainty and randomness are mathematically definable, it follows that computers can help you reduce your investing risks. Obviously, every investor tries to minimize uncertainty, or the risk of losses. The computer can help reduce risks in two ways. First, it provides a clear mathematical description of the risks associated with specific investments. Thus you're alerted to the sort of results you might expect before you invest your money. And by plotting historic price trends, the computer allows you to carefully time your market entry. To do this, computers use mathematical models. These are loaded into a computer from prepackaged programs and are used to statistically track performance and allow you to project expected returns.

Overall, the key functions for computer-aided investing are:

- Portfolio management
- Year-end capital gain/loss statements
- Evaluation of potential investments
- Timing decisions for purchase and sale

A well-selected set of applications programs can help you with all four of these, and at the same time help you be a successful investor.

Selecting Applications Programs

Applications software is the means for turning computer hardware into a business or personal tool. Besides the hardware, software is the most important consideration in making your computer productive. Unfortunately, many people who could benefit most from small computers haven't used such machines before and so might not recognize the importance of selecting software. *Careful selection is critical.*

A program that's generally useful and easy to use, to learn, and to understand is often called *user friendly*. The term is overused, sometimes incorrectly by software publishers eager to sell, but the concept is valid. Easy-to-use programs interact with the user by means of prompts, helpful comments, and a natural flow of information requests and required decisions. Such programs are especially important for people who are unable or unwilling to spend a large amount of time in learning to run and master the software. A powerful program not only solves complex programs quickly, but also lets you work with it almost immediately.

You'll probably want to buy three or four investment application programs, simply because no one program can meet all your needs. You should at least consider these applications:

- Portfolio managers
- Electronic spreadsheets
- Personal financial managers
- Data communications programs
- Tax preparation and planning programs
- Technical or fundamental analysis programs

When picking applications programs you need to consider several factors. Does the program display and print charts and graphs of the information? Is the program able to handle a significant number of stocks or other investments, and for what period of time? Will the portfolio program maintain appropriate records and tax information? Does the program require extensive information data and therefore require access to a database? Is the program flexible enough for your needs? Keep in mind that investing, even with a personal computer, requires a significant amount of your time. Most important, remember that the computer can't make investment decisions for you, no matter how powerful and sophisticated the software.

Criteria for Successful Use of Applications Software
The successful use of any applications program requires that it be easy to use, well-documented, reliable, and cost-effective. An easy-to-use program is marked by effective use of screen layout, remarks to users, and good documentation. A well-documented program performs as it's described. Reliable software won't "crash" because of your errors, but instead "traps" them and lets you try again. A cost-effective program offers solutions at a reasonable price.

Thoughout the rest of this book, application programs are described and evaluated. To make it easier to extract information, the format remains consistent from chapter to chapter. In each review, the author or manufacturer is identified, the computers that can run the program are listed, and the suggested retail price is given. (You can find the addresses of program manufacturers in Appendix D.) A description of the program and its application is also provided, as well as program comments.

Major program evaluations also include a graphic illustration of the software's strengths and weaknesses. Figure 2-2 shows how these evaluations are listed.

Figure 2-2. Software Evaluation Format

	Fair	Good	Very Good	Excellent
Ease of Use	☐	☐	☐	☐
Documentation	☐	☐	☐	☐
Reliability	☐	☐	☐	☐
Cost-effectiveness	☐	☐	☐	☐

In reviewing a new program, it's important to examine its helps and aids. Does it offer a menu or simple prompts that lead you through the software? Does the program automatically turn on and activate itself when you put the disk in the drive and turn on the computer? Do guides on the screen help you make decisions in moving to the next page of the program? Do screens of information offer explanations and prompts on specific items of interest, so that you don't have to continually refer to the documentation?

Have special function keys been implemented? Is the user's manual a few photocopied pages, or does it have color graphics and binders? Does it meet your needs? Is there any source of training on the applications package? Do you have to train yourself, and if so, are tutorial materials available or included in the set of manuals that you receive?

You'll find the answers to these questions in the multitude of product evaluations and reviews included in this book. Your buying decisions can be made with more information, and that information is easy to locate. It's all here, in one place.

Spreadsheets

Spreadsheets

Spreadsheets for Portfolio Management

One of the valuable uses of a computer is to store, retrieve, and display current and past information on the securities held in your portfolio and to calculate the return over a period of time.

Many investors have turned to readily available spreadsheet programs, such as *VisiCalc*, as an alternative to purchasing investment software packages. These investors have found that spreadsheet programs are relatively easy to use and offer the user a great deal of flexibility in setting up electronic worksheets to meet individual investment needs. Once a worksheet is set up, any changes in information can be quickly analyzed.

Data used in these electronic worksheets can be updated manually, or a communications package, such as *Teleminder* or *Dow Jones Spreadsheet Link*, can be used for automatic updating from an online stock market database.

Using the arrays of cells on a spreadsheet is a logical way to handle portfolio management. An *electronic spreadsheet* is a coordinated set of rows and columns. The intersection of a vertical column and a horizontal row in a spreadsheet creates a *cell*. A cell can contain either a label (text) or a value (a number or a formula). Formulas create relationships between values in specified cells.

Screen-oriented spreadsheet programs use the computer as a giant electronic worksheet where the user constructs a model using available internal memory. This memory imposes restrictions on the size of the worksheet that can be constructed.

With the ability to calculate the ratio of values held in several cells in an array, you're readily able to calculate financial ratios, dividend yields, and return on investment. Any electronic spreadsheet, from *VisiCalc* and *SuperCalc* to *Multiplan* or *Lotus 1-2-3*, has the ability to format a worksheet and create formula relationships between cells.

Dow Jones Spreadsheet Link

Company: Dow Jones & Company, Inc.
Computers: Apple II series, Apple Macintosh, IBM PC, IBM PC XT

Price: $249 (Apple II), $99 (all others)

Summary: The *Dow Jones Spreadsheet Link* tracks the data requested from the Dow Jones News/Retrieval service and transfers it directly to your spreadsheet. The program works with *VisiCalc, Lotus 1-2-3,* and *Multiplan.*

The *Link* reads stock symbols from your spreadsheet and arranges them into a downloading arrangement. The program then calls Dow Jones, extracts selective data, and drops it into the proper spreadsheet format. The *Link* comes with a generous supply of sample spreadsheets for *VisiCalc, Multiplan,* and *Lotus 1-2-3.*

The program can read high, low, and closing prices of the stock symbols specified on your spreadsheet. In addition to current Dow Jones stock quotes, the *Link* handles requests for historical quotes; information from the disclosure extracts available on Dow Jones; and analytical and historical data from Media General Financial Services, a Dow Jones database of earnings, dividends, and price-earnings ratios and stock prices for more than 3200 companies.

The IBM and Macintosh versions require *Dow Jones Straight Talk* (which costs $79) to transfer information from Dow Jones News/Retrieval into spreadsheet format.

This program may be worth the price if you require daily prices for numerous stocks and bonds.

Multiplan

Company: Microsoft Corporation
Computer: Apple II series, Apple Macintosh, CP/M-80 computers, IBM PC (128K), TRS-80
Price: $195
Summary: *Multiplan* is an extremely easy-to-use electronic worksheet program. The program provides the user with 16,065 cells, or work locations, in 63 columns and 255 rows, each of which may contain words, numbers or mathematical formulas.

Multiplan's worksheet screen, or window, displays 140 cells at a time (7 columns × 20 rows); as many as eight separate windows or sections of the worksheet may be active at once. A cursor shows the location of the active cell on the worksheet and may be easily moved from cell to cell using the computer's arrow keys. (In the Macintosh version, the mouse is used.) Other simple commands allow the user to move from one section of the worksheet to another, and the Control-Q or Home command moves the cursor back to the top-left cell from any location on the worksheet.

In addition to the active window of the worksheet, the screen displays a command line listing the commands currently available, a comments line, and a status line. The status line identifies the active cell on the screen (R1C1 for instance), the amount of memory space remaining, and the name of the worksheet. *Multiplan* provides for the creation of an unlimited number of worksheets in separate files, and allows linking of several worksheets to speed data entry and editing. The SYLK (Symbolic Link) File Format system also allows communication between the *Multiplan* worksheet and other software packages.

Figure 3-1. *Multiplan*

	Fair	Good	Very Good	Excellent
Ease of Use	☐	☐	☐	☑
Documentation	☐	☐	☐	☑
Reliability	☐	☐	☐	☑
Cost-effectiveness	☐	☐	☑	☐

Comments: *Multiplan* is a flexible and powerful software program. It's very easy to use. The worksheet screen is well-organized and designed to aid the user in the completion of each operation.

The command line at the bottom of the screen lists all the available commands, and any one may be ordered simply by typing its first letter. Once a command has been chosen, it then appears on the command line along with a list of subcommands relating only to that command. Further, the program provides a Help command which lists and describes in detail any command or operation available. After reviewing the instructions for a selected command, you simply type R for Resume to return to the original worksheeet.

The *Multiplan* instruction manual is also well-organized and easy to follow. It's divided into two sections: a seven-chapter tutorial on the use of the program and a detailed reference guide to the system. The appendix to the instruction manual includes a complete glossary and a list of helpful hints for the advanced user. A 15-page quick reference guide is included with the package.

Multiplan has the ability to name cells. Therefore you can calculate Profits = Sales − Costs by referring to the cells previously named Sales and Costs. The ability to link worksheets is an effective advantage. It allows you, for example, to summarize on a new worksheet the results of individual worksheets.

Multiplan was the first independent product shipped for the Macintosh. Microsoft's established spreadsheet underwent a renovation to accommodate the advantages of the Macintosh before it was released in January 1984. It's still the best—and the most widely used—professional spreadsheet available for the Mac.

Financial Fastrax

Company: Integrated Equity Planning
Computer: Apple II series (CP/M required), IBM PC, IBM PC XT, IBM PC AT, IBM PC-compatibiles, Osborne
Price: $60 per volume (two volumes available)
Summary: A collection of financial analysis tools designed to work with *Lotus 1-2-3* or *SuperCalc*. It permits you to plan Individual Retirement Accounts, rate of return on investments, loans, and investment analysis.

The financed planning templates include Educat, a model for making projections of future college costs and the investments required to meet the costs. Educat can be used to project needs for any large predictable capital investment. It makes projections of your investments, determines shortfalls to meet the specified goal, and determines what lump sum or annual investment would be necessary to meet that goal. The model can simultaneously handle up to three different kinds of investments with different tax consequences and growth rates. By changing the assumptions, you can converge on an investment strategy that meets whatever goal you've chosen. This feature is perhaps the most valuable because it gives you the capability of coming up with a plan which can be altered later.

The section on investment analysis gives you three models to track how well you are doing with your investments—Stock, Bonds, and T-bill. Stock tracks a portfolio and calculates gain/loss, percent simple and compounded gains, and classifies the gain/loss as short- or long-term, based on the number of days held (which the model also computes). The model may be used for simple record keeping or as a planning tool. Bonds calculates price, yield to maturity, coupon payment amounts, and current yields. And T-bill allows you to determine what alternative investments would be needed to match a T-bill with characteristics you input.

Also available are spreadsheets that determine your qualifications for a loan, international currency conversions, and precious metals evaluation.

Spreadsheet Portfolio Evaluator
The *Spreadsheet Portfolio Evaluator* is a program using *SuperCalc* on an IBM PC to construct a worksheet to keep track of the performance of both individual stocks and a portfolio of stocks. It can be readily adapted to *Lotus 1-2-3* or advanced *VisiCalc*.

Spreadsheet Portfolio Evaluator uses three tables: capital gains or losses, dividend payments, and yields and returns. Table 1 calculates gain or losses, changes in stock prices, and changes in the value of the portfolio. Table 2 tracks the dividends for each of the stocks, while Table 3 calculates the yield on the purchase price and the total return on each stock.

Information on a single stock appears in a row and additional stocks can be readily added.

You have complete control over the electronic spreadsheet. If you want to calculate the weighted beta for your portfolio, insert some columns and enter the necessary formulas. If you want to use Standard & Poor's 500 stock index instead of the Dow Jones Industrial Average as a benchmark for performance, you can. If you want, you can modify the formulas to reflect the average commission you pay, or, if your broker's commission is particularly straightforward, you can create a lookup table that includes it directly in the calculations.

The *Spreadsheet Portfolio Evaluator* first appeared in an article by A. T. Williams in the *AAMI Journal*, Mar/Apr 1984, pp. 2–9. A copy of the *Portfolio Evaluator* may be obtained for $10 from Box 9563, Berkeley, CA. 94709. Specify *SuperCalc 2*, *SuperCalc 3*, or *Lotus 1-2-3*.

4

Telecommunications and Financial Databases

Telecommunications and Financial Databases

A growing number of people are using a personal computer to access financial information from remote electronic libraries called *databases*. A database is an online system which contains huge amounts of data. In many cases, the kinds of material stored in a database resemble lists, tabulations, and sets of numbers.

Databases which contain information regarding stocks, bonds, commodities, and financial information can be accessed by a computer user via the telephone lines. In order to obtain data from a financial database you need to convert your personal computer to a smart communications terminal, which then can communicate with a host (database) computer, and using your disk drive(s), record the information sent by the database onto your disks for later analysis.

You'll use a *modem* to communicate with the host computer. Modem is taken from the words *modulate* and *demodulate*, which notes the conversion of sound to digital data, and back again. Modems transmit this digital information back and forth over the telephone lines, usually communicating at 300 bits per second (bps) or 1200 bps. Transmission at 300 bps is roughly equivalent to sending 30 characters per second; 1200 bps is four times faster.

Although many modems contain the rudiments necessary to properly communicate with a database service, most users prefer the convenience, flexibility, and power of separate telecommunications software. These programs tend to fall into three categories:

- General-purpose packages which enable you to communicate with nearly any database system
- Communication modules included with investment software that give you access to one or a few database vendors
- Packages distributed by database services and designed specifically to access their products

Many programs store phone numbers and system configurations which can be called through simple menu selection. Log-on procedures for database services can also be stored and recalled through function keys. The ability to receive and print data simultaneously is often useful.

Most private investors want to use a financial database service to get stock price and volume information in order to update their portfolio or to follow the market for stocks of interest. The typical cost to update a stock portfolio might range from $10 to $50 per month when you use a financial database. Many portfolio management and stock analysis programs have automatic log-on features which allow stock quotes to be retrieved unattended so that you can access the database when the rates are lowest, normally after business hours. If you're spending a few hours a week entering data by hand now, the time saved by using a database and modem might well be worth the cost involved.

Typically, a financial information service has a subscription charge, as well as a minute by minute rate for using the system. There are significant savings when you use a service during nonprime hours in the evening and weekends.

The use of online electronic databases is growing and may grow even more rapidly as rates go down and ease of access improves. Information transferred to your computer has some distinct advantages over information you glean from reports, newspapers, and other printed sources. Since it's already in your computer, you can manipulate it much more readily, without having to rekey it in. Statistical information—stock quotes, for example—can be loaded directly into your favorite integrated spreadsheet or other appropriate program.

Business Computer Network
Company: Business Computer Network
Price: Subscription charges $50 per year or $5 per month, plus $.20 or $.25 per successful database access.
Summary: Business Computer Network has 16 online databases which include I.P. Sharp, MJK Commodities, Securities Data Service, General Electric Information Service, EasyLink, and Dialog.

You can use a program supplied by Business Computer Network called *SuperScout* with the IBM PC or PC-compatibles for accessing the network. Business Computer Network will also sell you a modem at a bargain price. This is an excellent, low-cost means of access to a collection of useful databases.

CompuServe

Company: CompuServe

Price: Starter Kit, which includes five hours of contact time, is $40. Contact charges are $6 per hour evenings and $12.50 per hour prime time. Some quotation programs have additional transaction charges.

Summary: You can access a wide number of databases including those for news, weather, and sports from major newspapers and international news services; current and historical financial information; corporate profiles; money market and commodities information; financial reference; and electronic banking.

Quick Quote gives you quick, easy access to regularly updated quotes on the ticker symbols you specify, as well as high and low prices, closing price, change since the prior day's closing price, and number of shares traded. Each current quote costs $.02 in addition to connect time.

Through News-A-Tron you can obtain current day quotations on key portions of the commodities marketplace and analysis of activity in the markets. These reports are updated periodically throughout the day.

The Standard & Poor's information file contains a summary, important developments, product line contributions to profits, corporate officers, and selected financial items for over 3000 companies. There's a $.25 charge for each company accessed.

Micro Quote permits you to see trading statistics and descriptive data on over 32,000 stocks, bonds, mutual funds, warrants, and options. Historical prices and volumes are available for most stocks back to January 1, 1974. Only current options are maintained.

Dow Jones News and Quotes Reporter

Company: Apple Computer, Inc.

Computer: Apple II series, IBM PC

Price: $135

Summary: Investors can obtain news, prices, and financial information on their investments easily with the *Dow Jones News and Quotes Reporter*. This program turns any Apple II or IBM PC computer into a smart terminal with access to a broad range of financial and general news information from the Dow Jones News/Retrieval database service.

The *Reporter* package contains one disk with the program, the operating manual for the program in spiral bound format, and a copy of the Dow Jones News/Retrieval *Fact Finder*. The *Fact Finder* is the 198-page Dow Jones publication which provides the instructions and symbols necessary to access and use the various portions of the database. The *Dow Jones News and Quotes Reporter* has a customizing feature that allows you to store on disk all the necessary information to dial automatically and log on to the service. This communication-assistance program can be very useful for those who frequently use Dow Jones News/Retrieval.

Dow Jones News/Retrieval

Company: Dow Jones News/Retrieval
Price: Standard rates are $72 per hour (prime time) and $12 per hour (nonprime time). The Executive Plan requires a $50 per month minimum, but charges $48 per hour and $7.80 per hour for prime and nonprime time respectively.
Summary: Dow Jones News/Retrieval is a comprehensive collection of business, financial, and general news databases. One database, Dow Jones News, has information on over 80 news categories, 7000 U.S. and Canadian companies, and 60 industries. News extracts are also provided from the pages of the *Wall Street Journal, Barron's*, and the Dow Jones News Service. You can find headlines that were just written or that were printed up to five years ago.

A text-search utility can use any combination of words or dates to search for news stories as far back as June of 1979. For example, by typing the words "bankrupt" and "steel" you'll find articles related to financially weak steel companies.

Dow Jones Quotes offers current (15 minute delay) and historical quotes and historical Dow Jones averages. Dow Jones Text Services will search the full text of the *Wall Street Journal* published since January 1984.

The financial and investment database offers timely earnings forecasts for 3000 of the most widely followed companies, as well as Disclosure, which contains 10,000 extracts and company profiles.

For subscribers seeking investment statistics, Media General, a popular financial database, provides information on the earnings, dividends, price-earnings ratios, and stock price performance relative to marketing indicators for 3200 companies listed on the New York, American, and over-the-counter exchanges. The database consists of two segments: companies and industry groups. Each segment can be easily searched by price and volume data, such as stock price action; and by fundamental data, such as earnings, dividends, and shareholdings.

Dow Jones News/Retrieval also supplies Standard & Poor's Online, which contains concise profiles of more than 4600 companies, including business summaries, recent market activity, and dividend information. Other useful financial and economic databases include Zacks Investment Research's Corporate Earnings Estimator, which provides earnings forecasts for 2400 companies; Money Market Services' Weekly Economic Survey, which features forecasts on changes in key economic indicators such as weekly money supply and federal funds rates; and the Merrill Lynch Research Service, which highlights reports prepared by Merrill Lynch's Security Research Division.

Dow Jones News/Retrieval also offers electronic mail through MCI. In addition, the service offers general databases such as movie reviews, sports reports, weather tables, and "Wall $treet Week" transcripts from the popular television program.

With the exception of commodities information, the Dow Jones News/Retrieval offers the investor a comprehensive collection of business and financial information. It's expensive, but if utilized fully you could save a tremendous amount of research time and make more-informed investment decisions, ultimately making it well worth the cost.

Dow Jones Reporter
Company: International Business Machines
Computer: IBM PCjr (128K memory)
Price: $100
Summary: The *Dow Jones Reporter* is a telecommunications package that enables your PCjr computer to act as a terminal to a large mainframe computer. The program provides the appropriate commands to enable the two computers to talk to each other, send messages back and forth, and to transfer data. *Dow Jones Reporter*, like any good communications program, sets up the connection automatically and requires no

prior knowledge of telecommunications. Once connected, you can access Dow Jones News/Retrieval.

This program is very similar to the *Dow Jones News and Quotes Reporter* package discussed earlier.

Duns Plus
Company: The Dun & Bradstreet Corporation
Computer: IBM AT, IBM XT (256K and 10M hard disk)
Price: $1,300
Summary: Including *Duns Plus, Lotus-1-2-3,* and the *Multimate* word processor, this integrated package allows you to access Dun's Financial Profiles, Dun's Quest, Dun & Bradstreet Computing Services, as well as commercial databases like the Official Airline Guide, Dow Jones, NewsNet, and The Source. Electronic mail is possible through Western Union.

The price includes the three pieces of software, documentation, one year of updates, and subscriptions to the various databases. Dun & Bradstreet also sells a complete system—IBM XT computer, training, installation, hardware, and software—for $10,200.

Financial Xchange
Company: Interactive Data Corporation
Computers: Apple II series, IBM PC
Price: Dependent upon the amount and type of data required
Summary: *Financial Xchange* provides access to databases of price and descriptive information for financial markets and broker's estimates of projected stock earnings. Extensive data for the stock and bond markets is provided.

FutureSource
Company: Commodity Communications Corporation
Computers: Apple II series, IBM PC
Price: $149 per month (Apple), $199 per month (IBM), plus exchange fees that average approximately $45 per month
Summary: A database and quotation service for commodity trading. Ten preselected pages allow you to format the quotes on contracts the way you want them to appear on your screen. With an Apple II you can create 16 intra-day, rescalable bar charts simultaneously and print them with your graphics printer. You can set your own high and low price limits for 32 individual contracts and your *FutureSource* system will alert you when your price objectives are met.

With the IBM PC you can obtain up to 23 different bar charts. You can display the last five trades and time of last trade of any futures contract. You get floor comments during market hours, government reports, and more. You can use the spread function to take realtime quotes and translate them into current spread quotes and view up to four functions on the screen at the same time.

FutureSource lets you switch back and forth between online, realtime price quotes, and technical studies or other software programs.

Independent Investors Forum

Company: Independent Investors Forum
Price: $360 for one-year membership, plus $10 per hour connect time charges (average connect time charges, including Telenet access, is approximately $18 per hour)
Summary: Independent Investors Forum is a computer accessed, interactive, investment advisory service which provides research, makes recommendations, and allows users to discuss stock market investments in a conference-like setting through the host computer. Intended primarily for small investors, Independent Investors Forum allows members to ask questions, send messages, and post bulletins concerning proposed investments. In addition, the Independent Investors Forum retains only those items that are of interest to the user. The monthly user's guide keeps members up to date on latest Forum research reports, helping to minimize telephone connect charges.

The Forum is an advisory service that bases its advice on fundamental analysis, such as on an examination of a company's balance sheet and on the market for its products. Independent Investors Forum secures its information from the company financial reports filed with the Securities and Exchange Commission (SEC), Standard & Poor's price and earnings data, and SEC reports on corporate insider trading.

Knowledge Index

Company: Dialog Information Services, Inc.
Price: $35 sign-up fee, $24 per hour connect charge in nonprime time and weekends
Summary: This powerful research tool is an offspring of Dialog, a comprehensive, relatively expensive database.

Knowledge Index contains over twenty different databases on the subjects of business, electronics, and computers. Corporate News produced by Standard & Poor's News offers tabular information on over 9000 publicly held U.S. companies. Business Information discusses all aspects of business management and administration.

General news appears in Newsearch, which summarizes 1100 newspapers, magazines, and journals, and in Magazine Index, which abstracts 435 popular American magazines. Government News lists documents currently for sale by the U.S. Government Printing Office and also indexes federally produced research and technical reports. Other databases cover education, psychology, engineering, medicine, pharmacology, agriculture, and books in print.

Knowledge Index is a simple system to learn and operate. All commands are in English, even if some of the abstracts are not. This service is only available in nonprime time, but it *is* an excellent bargain.

It also has three databases for trade and industry, the legal field, and biology. These recent additions increased the total number of citations contained in all the databases to about 15 million.

This database system is a very effective tool for many investors who wish to follow trends in business and research topics related to investments.

Market Link

Company: Smith Micro Software
Computer: Apple Macintosh, IBM PC, IBM PC XT, IBM PC AT, IBM PC-compatibles
Price: $85
Summary: This program is an automatic communications connector to Dow Jones News/Retrieval or The Source. This menu-driven program provides automatic autodial connection by modem and will automatically fetch quotes for up to 120 securities at up to eight user-predefined periods. This allows you to maintain up-to-date quotes and keep abreast of market news. The program works on a preset basis and you don't need to be there while it's running. *Market Link* can also interface with *Lotus 1-2-3* (on the PC computers), as well as with Smith Micro's *Stock Portfolio System* (see Chapter 6 for details of this package).

MicroDisclosure

Company: Disclosure
Computer: IBM PC (128K), IBM PC XT
Price: $45, plus $1 per minute access time
Summary: A database access program which offers key facts and figures on over 9000 public companies which are required to file with the Securities and Exchange Commission.

You can search by company name, geography, profits, sales, ticker symbol, number of employees, or 86 other categories. Then if you wish, you can download the balance sheets and the annual or quarterly income statements of one or more companies for offline analysis.

Micro/Scan

Company: Isys Corporation
Computers: Compaq, IBM PC, IBM PC XT, IBM PC AT
Price: Price varies, starting at approximately $6,000 per year
Summary: *Micro/Scan* is a set of databases available to professional investment managers and trust departments. Its prepackaged investment databases on monthly disks offer professional investment managers access to current data on as many as 7500 publicly held companies. With *Micro/Scan*'s set of integrated software programs (screening, sorting, ranking, portfolio analysis, report writing, data transfer to spreadsheets, statistics, histograms, and telecommunications), the databases can be screened or manipulated in virtually endless ways to produce detailed research which may lead to sounder, more profitable investment decisions. (For subscribers to more than one *Micro/Scan* database, the report writer software allows for merging data from multiple databases into a single report.)

You can create any number of personally-designed screen formats and printed reports to explore new investment strategies, test "what if?" projections, perform in-depth industry and portfolio analysis, or conduct acquisition searches.

The *Micro/Scan* database is updated monthly with new disks containing current pricing, earnings, dividend, and classification data as well as precalculated data ratios, depending on the database. If more frequent updating is desired, the Isys One/Source telecommunications service is available. It provides current prices and updates 18,000 data items on your disk in under five minutes over regular telephone lines. One/Source is available on a daily, weekly, or demand basis.

(*Micro/Scan*'s capabilities as a fundamental analysis tool are discussed in greater detail in Chapter 7.)

NaturalLink

Company: Texas Instruments, Inc.
Computer: TI Professional (256K)
Price: $150
Summary: *NaturalLink* provides simplified, automatic access to Dow Jones News/Retrieval from the Texas Instruments Professional computer. *NaturalLink* provides an easy-to-use method for retrieving information from the Dow Jones database.

The program dials the phone, logs on, and even uses your password. It can then query the database with questions you've previously set up, store the resulting data, and get you offline in a fraction of the time you would need to complete the process manually. Obviously, this cuts your online costs.

NaturalLink's best feature is that it enables you to build English-like questions that are then converted by the software into the cryptic commands used by Dow Jones.

NaturalLink uses a series of windows, each containing a list of words or phrases for a portion of a command. After you choose one of the available options, a new menu is displayed, based on the selection. In this way you build an English sentence which can be submitted to the computer as a command with a single press of the Enter key.

You can personalize *NaturalLink* by building a stock portfolio containing up to several hundred companies. With such a list, you can easily access the financial information found in the 22 databases of Dow Jones News/Retrieval.

NewsNet

Company: NewsNet
Price: $24 per hour prime time; $18 per hour nonprime time. Minimum monthly fee of $15; no signup fee.
Summary: NewsNet contains 154 electronic editions of newsletters such as the *Ford Investment Review* and the *Stanger Report*. However, it also contains newsletters from many other fields, such as the *CCH Tax Day* and the *Washington Credit Letter*.

Through the NewsFlash feature, every NewsNet subscriber can personally select up to ten words or complex phrases, which NewsNet will continually search for as new information enters its database. When NewsFlash locates matches for the words or phrases, you automatically get the headlines. You can read the full text of only those stories which are of interest. The charge to read the full text of an average article is about 50 cents. However, each newsletter establishes a reading cost in addition to the NewsNet access charge. These additional charges can add up if you access several newsletters each month. But if you copy the newsletter to your disk, you can read it *after* disconnecting.

NEXIS
Company: Mead Data Central
Price: Subscription $50 per month, plus $28 per connect hour
Summary: NEXIS includes research reports from Merrill Lynch, Paine Webber, and regional brokerage firms.

The database covers some 1500 companies in 100 industries. Nexis Exchange also carries the full text of SEC filings by those corporations. Currently, 10-Q reports, 10-K, and 8-K filings are available.

There are full-text articles from more than 120 newspapers, magazines, professional and trade journals, and wire services. The online list of publications includes the *New York Times* and various business journals such as the *Harvard Business Review*. Originally available only to customers who leased Mead terminals, these services are now open to IBM PC users who purchase the necessary software from Mead.

One service that Mead provides is of particular interest to business users: a special abstract service covering advertising and marketing. Mead also markets LEXIS, a legal database that includes the full text of court decisions.

Nite-Line
Company: National Computer Network
Price: $30 signup (additional $45 for Apple II series or IBM PC conversion disk), plus $20 per hour (300 bps); $26 per hour (1200 bps) during daytime, plus database use charge ($4–$6 per hour); evening and night charge is $9 per hour (300 bps), $5 per hour (1200 bps)
Summary: Nite-Line provides access to financial databases for options, stocks, and commodities, as well as the Media General Market file data.

You may request specific financial data for a desired date or range of dates. Nite-Line retrieves the data and transmits it (at either 300 or 1200 bps) to your computer, where it's collected on its disk or tape drive. You then disconnect from Nite-Line and use the data offline in your own programs.

PC Quote
Company: PC Quote, Inc.
Computers: IBM PC, IBM PC XT, IBM PC AT, PC-compatibles
Price: $245 per month, plus exchange fees ranging from $5 to $90 per month
Summary: Until recently, the brokerage houses and the floor traders at the various exchanges enjoyed an advantage over the serious investor working without access to the high-speed ticker. Brokers and traders watched the market change and the "tick." They took advantage of this information. When their security moved, so did they.

Now the portfolio manager, fund manager, or active investor can be just as current as the brokerage firms or floor traders. The moment a price change occurs on an exchange, it changes on the PC Quote screen.

There are several advantages to the system. PC Quote delivers last sale information. It monitors 18 securities on each screen (which can be changed at any time) and automatically displays current last sale prices. The program monitors the bid/ask market. It displays last sale, time of last sale, change for the day, size of the bid/ask, and time of the bid/ask. All data is current with the tick. PC Quote provides realtime portfolio evaluation. It also provides limit minders informing you when a security has reached the high or low limits you've previously defined. PC Quote will continue to update prices and will provide a constant monitor line, which displays a specific security no matter where you are in the system. The program monitors securities on nine major exchanges and allows you to select 60 securities for the last sale or bid/ask monitors.

PC Quote is not a dial-up service, but instead provides information by satellite. A small (two-foot wide) satellite dish is included in the monthly charge.

Personal Investor

Company: PBL Corporation
Computers: Apple II series, IBM PC
Price: $70
Summary: The *Personal Investor* is a software package designed to connect to Dow Jones News/Retrieval or other electronic news services. This program also allows you to maintain an investment portfolio on specific stocks. To help maintain the investment portfolio, there is a "cursor calculator" which does the four math functions while data is being entered. There's also a word editor that allows text to be inserted or deleted.

There are several types of reports which can be generated by the *Personal Investor*: tax reports, description and price reports, gain/loss reports, and dividend reports.

Personal Investor has three functions: retrieve business news, update a portfolio, and collect quotes on preassigned list of securities.

- The News/Terminal automatically signs on to Dow Jones, giving access to the *Wall Street Journal, Barron's,* Dow Jones news, and 50 key financial indicators on 3200 selected companies. The News/Terminal is also compatible with most other terminal services. Incoming text can be viewed through a 40-column window in either 40- or 80-column format, and a printer can easily be turned on and off.
- The Portfolio Manager generates four reports which include information on individual stock purchase and total portfolio gains/losses, sale of stock with profits/losses, dividend yields on purchase and current price, and dividend date. Sales and purchase expenses such as commissions are reported. Multiple purchases of the same stock are accounted for individually. Each stock is updated by the Dow only once. Stock splits are calculated automatically and recorded. The Portfolio Manager can be manually updated.
- Quotes on preassigned stocks can be quickly collected, then viewed at leisure offline. Quotations include Bid and Ask; Yesterday's Closing Price; Today's Opening, Highest, Lowest, and Last Price; Trading Volume; and Current Dividend Yield. The New Change from Yesterday's Close to Last Price is also reported.

Personal Investor is a well-respected portfolio manager program with added features that give easy access and updating through electronic databases. The program is well-constructed and documented, and is definitely easy to use.

pfs: Access
Company: Software Publishing Company
Computers: Apple II series, IBM PC, IBM PC XT
Price: $70
Summary: A communication program for accessing any publicly available database service. With a keystroke you can connect with CompuServe, Dow Jones News/Retrieval, MCI Mail, The Source, and Western Union EasyLink services. You can also customize the menu by adding or substituting services with selections of your choice.

This program also provides the ability to encrypt files you may send to an electronic mailbox.

Quotdial
Company: Quotron Systems, Inc.
Price: $50 initial fee. Connect charges of $30 (prime time) or $10 (nonprime time) under Option A. Option B charges are $150 per month, with access charges of $6, $8, or $11 per hour, depending on proximity to Telenet access mode.
Summary: Quotdial offers both a realtime and an after hours source of market data. This includes stock, bond, option, stock index, financial futures, and commodities prices. Quotdial also provides access to leading market indicators, the most actively traded issues, a recap of advancing and declining issues, pertinent dividend and earnings information, and earnings forecasts.

The after market hours service is available from 15 minutes after the market closes until approximately two hours prior to the next day's market opening. Market statistics, option displays, and graphic displays are all available with Quotdial.

Scanset
Company: Matra Communication
Price: $895
Summary: If you don't have a personal computer, nor need one, you might consider purchasing a Scanset terminal for accessing informational services and databases. The Scanset

plugs into your phone line and has six programmable function keys, as well as a built-in phone. The Scanset XL's programmable keys are the heart of the machine. They allow you to store up to 122 of those hard-to-remember log-on sequences and computer commands in the terminal's memory. Scanset XL provides you with automatic log on, automatic dialing of up to 36 phone numbers, and one-button access to the databases. You can even use the phone while information is being retrieved.

The Scanset has a built-in modem, 9-inch display, and 69-key keyboard.

SEC Online
Company: SEC Online, Inc.
Price: $57 per hour prime time, $46 per hour nonprime time (after 7:30 p.m.)
Summary: A database of the original reports which public companies file with the Securities and Exchange Commission (SEC). These reports include the annual report, the proxy statement, the 10-K, 10-Q, 8-K, and 20-F reports. Also included in the system are company research reports and corporate releases.

You can read the report online, print it on your printer, transfer to a disk, or order a hardcopy which will be shipped to you.

Securities Data
Company: Securities Data Access, Inc.
Price: $4 per contract and $5 per stock for one year's information
Summary: This company provides historical data on commodities, stocks, bonds, options, and mutual funds. They provide the data on a disk in your selected format, such as *Lotus 1-2-3*, *Compu Trac*, and *CSI* for the Apple II series and IBM PC. The commodity data provides the open, high, low, settlement, and volume for each day for $4 per year. The stock data includes high, low, close, and volume. This is a low-cost way to obtain historical data for spreadsheet and other programs.

The Source
Company: The Source Telecomputing Corporation
Price: Registration fee of $49.95, plus $20.75 per hour (prime time) or $7.75 per hour (nonprime time)

Summary: The Source contains 47 information databases and 12 electronic communication services, representing nearly 800 specific services. The databases are categorized under News, Weather, and Sports (including access to up-to-the-minute international, national, and local news from United Press International); Business and Investing; Communications Services; Personal Computing; Travel Services; and Shopping, Games, and Leisure.

Using the Stockvue service you can access more than 55 items of information on over 3100 common stocks from the New York, American, and over the counter exchanges. Each of these items is updated weekly by Media General, Inc., of Richmond, Virginia. An additional surcharge is required for Stockvue.

The Source makes it possible to keep up with the latest business trends by providing abstracts of leading financial publications through Management Contents, Ltd. In addition, information from the Commodity News Service wire is available. A variety of other services are available including computer conferencing, electronic mail, UPI news, and a travel service.

If you just want a stock quote, you can bypass the menu and go directly to Stockcheck. There you can get a quote (delayed 15 to 25 minutes) on any of 10,000 securities. There's no extra charge for this.

Through Spear Securities, The Source offers online trading at discount commission rates. The entire process of order entry, stock transaction, and online confirmation takes only two minutes. An automated portfolio tracking system also follows the values of your securities and provides loss and gain statements. Current (last trade) quotes are offered, at a higher cost ($20 per month surcharge), as well as the less expensive quotes delayed approximately 20 minutes.

STC/SSI Investor Services (described in Chapter 5), offered via The Source, offer additional investment databases. Presently included in the system are the Media General Financial Service for historic stock analysis; Commodity World News; The Donoghue Financial/Investment Newsletter; the electronic *Washington Post*; and Bizdate, The Source's own electronic business magazine that's updated around the clock, every weekday.

A new service begun in March, 1985, Investext is a database offered on The Source which provides full-text research reports from 27 domestic and 11 foreign investment firms. The research includes financial data, analysis, and recommendations for 2500 U.S. and 1500 foreign companies, 50 industry groups, and 1000 products. Investment firms such as Kidder, Peabody & Co., Smith Barney, and E.F. Hutton contribute reports. You can search Investext by company, industry, stock symbol, product, report number, or SIC code. Hourly rates are $40 evenings and weekends, $45 weekdays. Additional surcharges for each report average $45–$90.

Stockpak II
Company: Standard & Poor's Corporation
Computers: Apple II series, IBM PC
Price: Composite set of 1500 leading companies $275 per year, or all NYSE (1500 companies) $275 per year, or all OTC (2200 companies) $520 per year
Summary: With *Stockpak II*, investors are able to review key financial information on up to 4500 companies, graphically compare and analyze information on groups of companies, and perform simple or complex searches to locate specific types of companies. More than 100 information items are available for each company in the database, such as stock ranking, earnings, dividends, sales, price history, and performance ratios. The system consists of a program disk and one database disk for either the NYSE, AMEX, or OTC markets. A market composite disk with data for over 1500 firms is also available. Monthly database updates are included in the subscription fees.

Investors can perform functions such as searching for a company's financial profile or graphing multiple profiles on a singe screen. A searching function allows screening by total sales, assets, and other financial parameters for fundamental analysis.

Teleminder and Tele-Pak
Company: Teleware, Inc.
Computers: Apple II series, Apple III, IBM PC
Price: $195 (*Teleminder*), plus $30 (*Tele-Pak*)
Summary: *Teleminder* is a sophisticated communications program for use in retrieving news stories, stock prices, and other

information from Dow Jones News/Retrieval. Once the program is set up, it can automatically dial the telephone (through an appropriate modem), connect to Dow Jones, and retrieve all the current stories and current stock prices of interest. In addition, when the computer is equipped with an internal clock, *Teleminder* may be programmed to retrieve news and stock quotes at a specified time each day, or each week. Once the clock is set, all you have to do is leave the computer on and the program automatically retrieves the desired information at the preset time and stores it on a disk.

Teleminder is menu-driven, with a main menu and a utilities menu. Selections on the main menu allow you to create, change, and delete a list of stock prices or news stories, retrieve information immediately or set up for timed retrieval, and to communicate with the Dow Jones. You may designate a particular list on a disk as either active or inactive. When the system is connected to the Dow Jones, only those items on the active lists are updated. Selections on the utilities menu allow you to establish system parameters, format data disks and stock quote disks, set the international clock, and print quotes and headlines. Each data disk can store up to 40 news stories and 360 stock quotes. The stock quotes disk is designed to store only stock quotes, up to 1800 of them, transferred from a data disk.

Tele-Pak is a stock quotes utility program designed for *Teleminder*. *Tele-Pak* can be used to manipulate the current and historical stock quotes data so that it may be used as input to investment analysis and spreadsheet programs. The program transfers all current and historical quote files into a Data Interchange Format (DIF) for use by such programs as *Dow Jones Market Manager, Dow Jones Market Analyzer, Lotus 1-2-3,* and *Multiplan. Tele-Pak* also lets you print the historical and current quotes files stored by *Teleminder.*

Comments: *Teleminder* is an efficient and easy-to-use program for retrieving information from Dow Jones News/Retrieval. It's not as sophisticated a program as those which provide for technical or fundamental analysis of stock price data, as well as information retrieval, but it should be very useful for the investor who wishes to retrieve selected news stories and stock data for later analysis. The *Tele-Pak* utility provides an important function in allowing the user to transfer stock quotes to any of a number of other investment analysis programs.

Figure 4-1. *Teleminder* and *Tele-Pak*

	Fair	Good	Very Good	Excellent
Ease of Use	☐	☐	☐	☑
Documentation	☐	☐	☐	☑
Reliability	☐	☐	☐	☑
Cost-effectiveness	☐	☐	☑	☐

Teleminder is well-organized, with a simple-to-use menu system and good screen prompts. The program package includes the *Teleminder* master program disk, the *Tele-Pak* master program disk (at additional cost), a data disk, and an instruction manual. The manual is complete and detailed and has instructions for connecting to Dow Jones. The manual's appendix includes a list of error messages, a menu map, and suggestions for troubleshooting various problems. The program also comes equipped with a reference card.
Note: Although *Teleminder* and *Tele-Pak* are no longer available from Teleware, Inc., you may be able to find the packages in local computer stores or through mail order houses.

Tickertec
Company: Max Ule & Company, Inc.
Computer: Apple II+, CP/M computers, IBM PC, Northstar Horizon, TRS-80 Models II, 12, and 16 (all computers require an installed CP/M operating system).
Price: $1,950 (Standard *Tickertec* Version IV), $135 per month use rate. (Contact Max Ule for complete price list of options available.)
Summary: *Tickertec* is a highly sophisticated microcomputer-based computer program designed to provide extensive stock market quotation information. The system ties directly into the exchange quote ticker systems and provides realtime quotes for both the New York Stock Exchange and the American Stock Exchange. It's not a costly open-line telephone connection, but a special wire. It does not give OTC quotes because there is, at present, no OTC ticker.

The program restricts price and market information to clients of Max Ule & Company, a discount brokerage house. Ule also offers a trading service via CompuServe (see Chapter 5 for details on this service, called Tickerscreen).

Tickertec also includes a portfolio management module. The system can maintain one or more portfolios containing any number of securities, limited only by the amount of space available on a single disk. The module processes buy and sell orders (actually add or subtract securities from the portfolio), automatically updates current price information, reports the short and long positions, and reports current holdings. Each portfolio requires a separate disk file.

While the data that *Tickertec* continually accesses and displays is basic stuff of technical analysis, and while you can link your system to a printer and print out all the data continually displayed on the screen, the system does not generate charts.

Vickers On-Line

Company: Vickers Stock Research Corporation
Price: $50 per year, plus $1 per minute access charge
Summary: This database provides information on block trades, institution trades, SEC filings, and insider action. You can determine what professional money managers are buying and selling, and the change in their holdings. It's a complete database on over 4000 institutions holding stock, from pension funds through colleges. You can see their total portfolio, current positions, and changes over the last four quarters. You can view the activity of institutions trading a specific stock. Online screens include names, addresses, and telephone numbers of who to contact. With Vickers On-Line, you can select to find out who owns a stock (and who does *not* own your stock) in a given zip code range.

In addition, you'll have access to a database of valuable insider (officers and directors) information reported to the Securities and Exchange Commission including: 5 percent equity ownership (Form 13D); change in beneficial ownership of securities (Form 4); and notice of proposed sale of securities (Form 144). This enables you to see which insiders are buying and selling shares in their own company or companies they have an interest in. This information is added to the database within 48 hours of being received at the Securities and Exchange Commission in Washington, D.C.

VisiLink
Company: VisiCorp
Computers: Apple II series, Compaq, IBM PC, IBM PC XT
Price: $250, plus $10 for each Datakit.
Summary: Data Resources has one of the most extensive set of economic and financial databases available. For many years, it has been supplying financial database services and software to the nation's largest corporations. The company, cooperatively with VisiCorp, had marketed a database retrieval service which can be used by individuals and smaller companies. Called *VisiLink*, it's designed to supply specific financial or other data to personal computer users.

VisiLink was marketed by VisiCorp (VisiCorp is now out of business, but the program can still be purchased in many computer stores). With it you can log on to the Data Resources System and receive a customized report for the data of interest. Data retrieved can be loaded into *VisiCalc* spreadsheets for further analysis. Many customized data reports (called Datakits) are already available from Data Resources. The company can also create custom reports to fit specific needs.

There are three types of Datakits available to the *VisiLink* user: business analysis, investment analysis, and economics analysis.

Business analysis information supplies facts that affect one's business: cost indices, wholesale prices, and producer prices. There's also data on developments in 11 industries, including automotive, agriculture, and banking.

Investment-analysis data ranges from daily stock prices, interest rates, and commodities futures to foreign exchange rates.

Should you want to study an individual company, there's Standard & Poor's Compustat. This covers 5700 companies, with balance sheets, income statements, and fund sources. There's also FDIC data on some 14,000 banks, 3000 savings and loan firms, and 800 mutual savings banks. A.M. Best has also supplied financial statements on some 1900 insurance companies.

The economics analysis covers the U.S., Canada, Japan, major Central and Latin American countries, major Asian countries, and major European countries—all with historical and forecasting data.

VU/TEXT

Company: VU/TEXT Information Services

Price: $75 per hour (Option 1), $100 per hour (Option 2). Additional charges vary and depend on database accessed.

Summary: VU/TEXT is a nationwide database system for searching and retrieving the text of selected newspapers and the information in selected business information services. VU/TEXT was originally designed as an in-house online database for reporters and editors at the *Philadelphia Inquirer* and later the *Philadelphia Daily News*. It's now a full-service subscription database system available to newspapers, businesses, and the general public. The VU/TEXT system provides text from several newspapers, including the *Washington Post* and the *Wall Street Transcript*, and several general and business databases, including the *Academic American Encyclopedia* database and the Prompt database produced by Predicasts, Inc.

Other VU/TEXT databases of interest to investors include the AP wire, the PR wire (public relations material placed on a wire by companies), Commodities (10-minute delay), and especially VU/QUOTE, which presents NYSE, the American Stock Exchange, and NASDAQ (over-the-counter) quotes with the standard 15-minute delay.

Access to the VU/TEXT system is available through the Telenet telecommunications network. Once the VU/TEXT system is online, you simply select the database and begin a search. In the newspaper databases, a search may be conducted according to a keyword or phrase, or according to one of eight fields. These field types include the article's date, publication, page and edition, byline, section, and headline. Once a search is completed, the text found may be displayed on the screen or printed out. In the business and general information databases, you must follow the search techniques specific to that database.

Warner Computer Systems

Company: Warner Computer Systems
Price: Initial sign-up fee of $48. Access charges average $30 per hour, depending on the service required.
Summary: Warner Computer Systems, Inc. is one of the major firms offering comprehensive financial information to investors. Through the company's seven databases, you can access a wide variety of information including:

- Descriptive and historical pricing, dividends, and earnings information on over 50,000 securities
- Current weekly and monthly prices for over 16,000 corporate bonds and selected municipal bonds
- Pricing information for all options
- Financial and management information on nearly 9000 publicly held companies through Disclosure II
- Consensus earnings forecasts for over 3000 companies through the Institutional Brokers Estimate System
- Fundamental information on over 6000 companies going back 20 years and 40 quarters through Compustat

Window On Wall Street

Company: Bristol Financial Systems, Inc.
Computer: IBM PC (256K)
Price: $1,295
Summary: *Window On Wall Street* is a package of programs which provide financial analysis tools combined with online (without delay) information from the New York Stock Exchange.

To accommodate varying needs, *Window On Wall Street* software is designed in a modular fashion. Minimum software required for operation is the *Base Software* which includes the Live NYSE Ticker, Select Ticker, Market Box Score, NYSE Quote Line, and Stock Watch. The *Portfolio Display and Valuation, Reports, Stock Alerts, Transaction Recall, Fundamental Data Library,* and *Customer Trading* are all options that can be added as required.

This program set includes a portfolio manager and a customer trading module useful for professional investment managers and stockbrokers.

Trading Securities by Computer

Trading
Securities
by Computer

As long as you own a computer, you can have instant access to stock quotations and the value of your portfolio. Once you have all that information, you usually pick up a telephone to call a brokerage office.

Now, however, a number of brokerage firms enable investors to execute stock trades directly—through computers. All you need is a modem and communications software (examples of the latter are listed in Chapter 4).

With a modem and software, you're able to place a buy or sell order from your computer to the stock broker's host computer. This allows you to place orders in the evening—these orders can then be executed by the broker at the first opening of the market.

C.D. Anderson

The discount brokerage firms of C.D. Anderson of San Francisco and Fidelity of Boston offer online trading via Trade Plus. (See Appendix D for addresses of these firms.)

C.D. Anderson offers the execution service through its *Desk Top Broker* system. Customers can buy and sell stocks, view portfolios, and monitor and track 18 selected stocks. A double-password system is used for security when buying and selling stocks.

Your initial investment for the system costs $50 for registration and software. Online charges range between $.10 per minute evenings and weekends and $.40 per minute during prime time. Software features include auto-dialing, pagination, and downloading information into spreadsheet programs.

The *Desk Top Broker* allows you to keep up to three portfolios on the system: a Personal, an IRA, and a Keogh. With three key strokes you can call up a portfolio, in which the securities reflect current value.

As soon as a trade's execution is confirmed, your portfolio is automatically updated to reflect the transaction. If the trade is a sale, the transaction is automatically entered into your tax records as well.

You can use an IBM PC, Apple II series, or any MS/DOS computer to connect to C.D. Anderson.

Fidelity Investor's Express

You can buy and sell stocks and options and specify a market order or orders with day or good-until-cancelled limits. These orders can use your margin or cash account via Fidelity's discount brokerage, utilizing the *Trade Plus* system. You can also view your portfolio record and track its performance.

When you trade a security, your portfolio and tax records are updated automatically. Of special interest is the fact that Investor's Express allows you to include all of your securities in your records, not just those purchased through the system.

Customers are able to transfer data for offline analysis to spreadsheet and graphics programs, including *VisiCalc, Multiplan*, and *Lotus 1-2-3*.

Prices for the Investor's Express service include a one-time subscription fee of $49.95 (includes one hour of connect time) and access charges of $.40 per minute during prime time hours and $.10 per minute during nonprime time, with a minimum monthly charge of $15. Investor's Express and the *Trade Plus* system are easy to use, and only minimal reference to the operating manual is needed.

With financial companies such as Fidelity and C.D. Anderson offering this kind of service, it's only a matter of time before other firms provide something along these lines. In fact, at the time of this writing, Charles Schwab, another discount brokerage house, had recently announced similar services.

Huttonline

The brokerage firm of E. F. Hutton introduced Huttonline in December, 1983. Huttonline enables clients to access Hutton's research and investment reports and read messages left for the client. The client can also access his or her account record and examine balances, portfolio records, recent transactions, and open orders. The client can then send a message to his or her Hutton account executive regarding an order.

Huttonline also provides a stock quote service for retail customers. Subscribers can access quotes for all securities and options and NASDAQ stocks from all national exchanges. The quote service provides the day's high, low, and closing price; trading volume; last sale; and net charge for all listed securities, options, and NASDAQ stocks. Quotes during market hours are delayed 20 minutes.

The system is menu-driven, and Hutton's clients will find it easy to use. The service is available (again, only to E.F. Hutton clients) for an initial charge of $25 and a monthly fee ($17 per month, plus $7.50 per hour access charges).

The system does not enable a Hutton client to directly execute an order. However, it *does* permit the client to access all the latest information and direct an account executive to execute an order. A client can access Huttonline using almost any personal computer.

Naico-Net

North American Investment Company, based in East Hartford, Connecticut, is a full-service broker which also offers home brokerage. North American sells a service named Naico-Net, which home computer owners can tie into through such online information systems as CompuServe and The Source. You can fill out an application with the firm right at the computer, without first ordering any software or making a telephone call.

Unlike the discount broker services, Naico-Net provides investors with advice and research on securities followed by the firm's analysts, and it doesn't limit its customers to stock and option trading. Naico-Net charges a commission lower than that charged by other full-service brokers.

The initial subscription fee is $20 and the online charges are $.28 per minute (prime time) and $.10 per minute (nonprime time).

For the price of the connect charges, North American's customers can obtain the company's research on stocks and tax information prepared by a major accounting firm. Quotes are available at extra cost. Customers are billed $.05 per quote, plus $.20 per minute above regular time charges. The system can bundle hundreds of price quotes for simultaneous delivery to the customer's computer.

North American customers can use sophisticated software housed in the firm's mainframe computer. For example, an options analysis package costs about $60 an hour. Other software is expected to be online soon.

Figure 5-1. Placing an Order

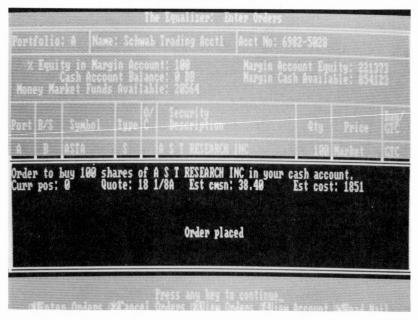

Placing an order to Schwab with the *Equalizer* is simple.

Schwab Equalizer

Company: Charles Schwab and Co., Inc.

Computers: Apple II series (128K), IBM PC, IBM PC XT, PC-compatibles

Price: $199 (additional online charges when accessing Dow Jones and Standard & Poor's Marketscope)

Summary: The *Equalizer* provides access to online trading and account information, as well as extensive research information. It provides comprehensive company profiles including earning forecasts, current outlook, price/volume charts, and financial history on most companies. It also has quotes, realtime when trading, otherwise delayed 15 minutes. *Equalizer* offers the latest company news from Dow Jones News/Retrieval, stories available in headline form for easy scanning or in full story form. Also available is Marketscope from Standard & Poor's reporting on market movements, "hot" stocks, even investment ideas—all online and accessible when you need them.

Online trading allows you to order directly. Notification and commission reports are placed in your personal electronic mailbox. Your portfolio is automatically updated, whether you place an order by phone or computer.

Spectrum
Company: Chase Manhattan Corporation
Computers: Apple II series, Commodore 64, Compaq, IBM PC, IBM PC XT, IBM PC AT, IBM PC-compatibles
Price: Monthly charges: Banking—$5; Video Broker—$5; Portfolio Manager—$6; Market Letter Digest—$4
Summary: Spectrum is an electronic banking and financial information service which provides delayed stock and option prices and a market newsletter. Using the Video Broker service, you may also place stock and option orders through Rose and Company. A portfolio tracking program organizes the portfolio, automatically entering the trades made. Spectrum also permits you to pay bills, keep tax records, and complete banking activities. The service uses a toll-free 800 number for access.

STC/SSI Investor Services
Company: The Source
Price: $49.95 subscription fee, plus a charge for connect time. An additional $20 per month for realtime quotes.
Summary: STC/SSI Investor Services are available by subscribing to The Source, the publicly available database service. You can obtain delayed stock quotes as part of the regular Source service or pay an additional $20 per month for realtime (instantaneous) stock quotes. The purchase and sell service is offered with Spear Securities of Los Angeles. When a trade is made, the client's entire portfolio, including tax records, is automatically updated.

Investor Services include such features as online securities trading and confirmation; realtime and delayed stock quotations; automatic portfolio updating and recordkeeping; and a variety of investment information databases. Some services charge more than the normal connect time rates. (See the description of The Source in Chapter 4 for more details on the entire database offerings.)

Tickerscreen

A New York discount brokerage firm, Max Ule & Company, originated the concept of placing orders by computer in 1982. Ule customers can reach the firm through the CompuServe information network. Orders are left on the system primarily at night for next trading day execution. Currently only orders to buy or sell at the market can be placed. Although orders are entered by computer, they are not for immediate execution.

Tickerscreen provides closing New York Stock Exchange stock prices, closing market indexes, commission computation on any stock or option transaction, and a demonstration of Tickertec, a stock market monitor. Tickerscreen is available 5:00 p.m. to 9:00 a.m. weekdays and 24 hours weekends. Clients who have brokerage accounts with Max Ule may leave orders on the system to buy or sell stocks for execution the following morning. This is free to Ule clients.

If you need up-to-the-minute stock information, Tickerscreen receives continuous data from the low-speed tickertape of the New York and American stock exchanges and flashes it across the bottom three lines of the computer screen.

Unisave

Unified Management of Indianapolis offers Unisave, which permits a personal computer to connect to Unified's discount brokerage system for account information, transactions, and investment research. A client has free access to all details and information about his or her account and communication by electronic mail to his or her Unified financial consultant. Clients are allowed free entry of mutual fund transactions, brokerage orders (with the standard Unisave commissions), and reviews of securities positions. The activity display shows all account activity shown first—current up to the very minute.

The Positions display provides complete information for all securities positions, including a money market account; and unified mutual funds, common and preferred stocks, bonds, and options. The display shows the name, trading exchange, purchase date, quantity, present custodian, current market price, market value, and a Unisave performance rating for all common stocks.

For open positions, the unrealized capital gains or losses are provided. For closed positions, the realized capital gains or losses may be reviewed.

You can enter (or cancel) brokerage orders for stocks, bonds, or options by personal computer at any time. During market hours, many orders are executed in less than one minute and confirmed while you're still connected.

You may access investment research reports for $15 per hour (prime time) or $10 per hour (evenings and weekends).

6

Portfolio
Management

Portfolio
Management

If you buy and sell securities and commodities frequently, then you need a way to record and retrieve the data on each transaction. For someone with a number of transactions, the requirement to produce all the records at tax time can be overwhelming. Using a portfolio management program to maintain a running record of your transactions will allow you to generate year-end reports, as well as meet the needs for information during the year.

Many portfolio management programs allow you to analyze your portfolio results against either the market as a whole or some sort of an ideal portfolio. Most can gather price information over telephone lines from Dow Jones News/Retrieval or one of the other online databases. Of course, you can still enter pricing information into these programs from the daily newspaper if you want.

In their most basic form, portfolio systems keep a record of each stock—buys, sells, commissions, dividends, and a current quote—so you can figure your open position. More sophisticated programs handle bonds, mutual funds, T-bills, and other cash equivalents. Most handle rights, warrants, and options.

Some even handle mortgage securities like Ginnie Maes. Besides giving you a picture of each investment you own, portfolio management systems give you a complete idea of your entire portfolio. They record a number of portfolios on each data disk, so you can maintain records of all your family's holdings or even track the results of several make-believe portfolios.

A number of portfolio management programs can provide you with a report, often arranged in various formats. Some of the programs have special features such as keeping track of the dates various options expire, or notifying you of investments that will soon become long-term. Others do tax accounting, so you can sell stock that will give you the greatest tax advantage at that time.

Many investors use portfolio management to track their securities in order to insure that interest and dividends are properly recorded, and to keep records of transactions for the IRS.

Figure 6-1. Portfolio Management

"I think my portfolio is nicely diversified—some electronics, rails, utilities, two cheese sandwiches and a slice of apple pie."

Courtesy of Sidney Harris

Generally, investors begin to see the advantages of a computerized system when they hold a portfolio of about 50 stocks and bonds, and have 30 or more transactions a year. Moreover, by using a portfolio management system, it's possible to set up both real and fictitious portfolios to test how various strategies work. You can also generate reports on capital gains and losses.

The limitations on most packages involve the number of stock characteristics maintained and/or computed for each stock (or other financial instrument). Most packages allow for a virtually unlimited number of stock records.

When you choose to update—on a daily, weekly, or other periodic basis—the program will perform certain automatic calculations, such as present value of the issues, or long- and short-term gains and losses (as if sold on that date). Finally, it will produce printable reports of your updated records.

It's possible to set up a portfolio manager using a spreadsheet or a program such as *T/Maker*. These programs enable you to set up tables of data on the securities and establish calculations of the performance of the portfolio.

Blu Chip
Company: XOR Corporation
Computer: IBM PC (128K), IBM PCjr (128K)
Price: $80
Summary: *Blu Chip* is a low-priced portfolio manager for stocks and other securities. It enables you to keep track of sales, purchases, dividends, and stock splits, as well as provide reports on the tax consequences of each transaction. The program includes a hypothetical portfolio that helps you learn to use the program, as well as a method for estimating a price in order to try alternative strategies.

Dow Jones Investment Evaluator
Company: Dow Jones & Company, Inc.
Computers: TI Professional
Price: $149
Summary: Intended for the investor with a limited number of stocks (less than 20), this program provides automatic-dialing access to Dow Jones News/Retrieval and also serves as a portfolio manager. The program comes with a sign-up application to Dow Jones (normally costing $50) and one free hour of time to get acquainted with the database's services.

Dow Jones Market Manager and Market Manager Plus
Company: Dow Jones & Company, Inc.
Computers: Apple II series, Apple III, Apple Macintosh (*Plus*), IBM PC (*Plus*), IBM PC XT (*Plus*)
Price: $299 (*Market Manager*), $249 (*Plus* for IBM), $199 (*Plus* for Macintosh)

Summary: The *Dow Jones Market Manager* is an investment portfolio data management and accounting system intended for the securities analyst, broker, small businessperson, and private investor. The *Market Manager* allows you to maintain a list of securities in an investment portfolio, update the information in this portfolio either manually or automatically (using Dow Jones News/Retrieval), and to prepare accounting and record keeping reports of portfolio holdings.

The types of securities accepted include common stocks, bonds, options, mutual fund shares, and U.S. Treasury issues. Transactions supported include buys, sells, short sells, and cash. Each data disk can hold up to 500 positions (or tax lots) in a single security or group of securities, and these 500 positions may be divided among as many as 26 different portfolios. The program may be set up so that it will automatically dial Dow Jones, retrieve and update the information in each security in the portfolio selected, and automatically disconnect.

The *Market Manager* prepares four kinds of printed reports: holdings by portfolio selected, holdings by security trading symbol, realized gains and losses by individual security, and year-to-date transactions. The last two reports may be particularly useful in choosing appropriate future transactions and in keeping tax records. In addition, when you make a closing transaction on any position in a portfolio, the program searches through the other current positions to see if there are sufficient holdings in the portfolio to match this buy or sell. You may then use this information to make an additional matching transaction or to add a new position to the portfolio.

Figure 6-2. *Dow Jones Market Manager*

	Fair	Good	Very Good	Excellent
Ease of Use	☐	☐	☐	☑
Documentation	☐	☐	☐	☑
Reliability	☐	☐	☐	☑
Cost-effectiveness	☐	☐	☑	☐

Comments: The *Dow Jones Market Manager* is efficient and easy to use. Menu-driven, it includes a main menu and six submenus (system setup, security pricing, portfolio maintenance, report generation, utilities, and communications). The *Market Manager* package includes a master program disk, a back-up program disk, a data disk, and a complete instruction manual. The manual contains a brief tutorial, a more detailed discussion of the process of connecting to Dow Jones News/ Retrieval, and a reference section. It also includes a list of error messages, a set of sample reports, and a map of the program menus.

One disappointment is *Manager's* inability to handle margin transactions. The program could also have been designed more efficiently. Delays of 15 to 20 seconds are not unusual as the program grinds its way from one module to another; the longest wait is about 40 seconds.

The *Market Manager Plus*, available in the first quarter of 1985, broadens the capabilities of the existing *Market Manager* software package by including new graphics and better charts. *Manager Plus* for the Macintosh also updates the portfolio management qualities of the *Market Manager* for easier access to financial information.

Invest
Company: Miracle Computing
Computer: IBM PC, IBM PC AT, IBM PC XT, IBM PC-compatibles (128K required)
Price: $250
Summary: *Invest* is a securities management and record keeping system designed primarily for the personal investor. It keeps records on a maximum of 650 portfolios of securities, with as many as 100 different categories or types of securities per portfolio. In addition, *Invest* provides for interest calculation by one of five different methods per category. These five methods include a daily variable rate method, a discount on principal yield method, simple and compound interest, and an optional, user-defined method. The program is menu-driven, with options for purchase, repurchase, sell, display, collect, report, and accrue interest, among others. *Invest* also provides for a "what if?" option which calls up a menu of 22 standard financial functions for use in analyzing a particular security or portfolio of securities.

These "what if?" functions include future value, annuity, nominal and effective interest rate, mortgage amortization, and municipal bond yield.

Figure 6-3. *Invest*

	Fair	Good	Very Good	Excellent
Ease of Use	☐	☑	☐	☐
Documentation	☐	☑	☐	☐
Reliability	☑	☐	☐	☐
Cost-effectiveness	☐	☑	☐	☐

Comments: *Invest* is a fairly simple program which functions primarily as a record keeping system for financial securities. The various financial functions available on the "what if?" menu act as a financial calculator, and are not directly integrated into the record keeping functions. *Invest* is fairly easy to learn and use, although the directions on the screen could be more detailed. The program comes with a detailed instruction manual which includes a brief tutorial on the use of each major option, as well as a reference section.

However, the instructions for starting the program for the first time and for copying the master disk were not very clear. Some experimentation is required to find the correct procedure. No quick reference card or other reference material is included with the program.

Note: The Payment Schedule option on the "what if?" menu would not accept data in any format for the city, state, and zip code entries, and when no data was entered, the program would send the user out of *Invest* and into IBM DOS. Upon typing LIST as a DOS command, the *Invest* program lines for this option would be printed, and upon typing RUN, the system returns control to the Payment Schedule option. Thus, the low mark in the Reliability category shown in figure 6-3.

Investor

Company: PCubed, Inc.
Computer: Apple Macintosh
Price: $150
Summary: A portfolio manager using the graphics and pull-down menus of the Macintosh. It produces reports titled Portfolio Status, Capital Gains/Losses, Interest Income, and Dividend Income. Security quotes are updated automatically via Dow Jones News/Retrieval. The powerful graphics capabilities of the Macintosh are used to chart the portfolio's performance.

Managing Your Money

Company: Micro Education Corporation of America
Computers: Compaq, IBM PC, IBM PC AT, IBM PC XT, Tandy 1200, (all require 128K and color graphics); IBM PCjr, Tandy 1000 (both require 256K)
Price: $200
Summary: *Managing Your Money* is a program for the management of personal finances. It takes an integrated approach to budgeting, tax programs, and checkbook programs. The portfolio manager is probably the most sophisticated part of this package, and the reason an investor should consider it. Not only does it track your portfolio, but it also enters the transactions into the tax module and sorts them out as long- or short-term capitol gains or losses, or as ordinary income. It also provides pie charts showing the profitable trades and unprofitable losses.

The portfolio manager can be used to track any security or commodity. You can use it to establish a trial portfolio (in other words, a simulation) to learn the results over time at no cost (or gain). The program, developed by Andrew Tobias, author of *The Only Investment Guide You'll Ever Need* (Bantam, 1983), is very useful for personal budget, investment tracking, and portfolio management.

Managing Your Money can handle a portfolio of 100 items with an IBM PC or other computer with 128K of memory. If your machine has 256K of memory, it can manage up to 500 items. Tobias's lucid, entertaining style appears throughout the prompts and help screens. The program handles short sells, stock splits, and stock dividends, and automatically notifies you of a stock becoming a long-term holding for tax purposes.

The software does not permit access of an online stock quote system, so prices must be updated manually. The *Managing Your Money* Financial Calculator computes compound interest, current yield, and yield-to-maturity on bonds; loan amortizations; after-tax cash flows; and internal rates of return.

Money Track

Company: Pacific Data Systems Corporation
Computer: IBM PC (128K, two disk drives, printer), IBM PC-compatibles
Price: $295
Summary: *Money Track* is a personal financial record keeping system designed for investors, accountants, business owners, and others who want to keep track of their investments, bank accounts, and other transactions. The program records simple financial transactions, such as writing checks or transferring funds from one bank account to another, as well as complex transactions involving a portfolio of stocks and bonds. *Money Track* is a menu-prompted system, with five major sections: transaction records, transaction reports, operations, additional procedures, and charts of accounts. You may record transactions in as many as 99 separate funds or major accounts, for 99 separate businesses, each with as many as 900 ledger accounts. Various types of printed reports are available, including a list of transactions, reports of individual funds, businesses and ledger accounts, and a chart of accounts. *Money Track* will also print checks in one of nine different formats. The program can store one year's set of transactions on a single disk, with a maximum storage size of 900 accounts per disk.

Figure 6-4. Money Track

	Fair	Good	Very Good	Excellent
Ease of Use	☐	☐	☑	☐
Documentation	☐	☐	☑	☐
Reliability	☐	☐	☑	☐
Cost-effectiveness	☐	☐	☑	☐

Comments: *Money Track* is an easy-to-use, yet fairly sophisticated financial management program. The main menu provides a clear guide to the variety of operations available and the system leads you through each specific operation with detailed directions on the screen. In addition, once a transaction has been entered, a command line appears and asks if you want the transaction sent to the file (File), restarted (Restart), or modified (Modify). If a necessary value has not been entered, the program prompts you to finish the entry. Only when all required entries have been made and the transactions balance (in a multiple distribution transaction) will the File command update the file. *Money Track* comes with a complete manual which includes many sample screen formats and detailed instructions on using each major program option. This manual also includes directions for starting the program for the first time, sample printed reports and checks, and a list of error messages. No quick reference card is included, though one's not really necessary considering the extensive screen directions.

Net Worth
Company: Bullish Investment Software
Computers: IBM PC, IBM PC XT, IBM PC AT, IBM PC-compatibles
Price: $60, plus $5 shipping via mail order from Bullish
Summary: *Net Worth* is a standard portfolio data management program for both the professional investor and the serious private investor. It's designed primarily to keep records of portfolio securities and transactions, and to report on these portfolios on a weekly basis. The program does provide for preparation of reports over periods longer than a week, but it's not intended to provide daily reports.

Net Worth maintains information for three separate types of data: portfolio accounts, account transactions, and securities information. In the portfolio accounts section, you may create and edit numerous investment portfolios consisting of holdings in stocks, bonds, precious metals, and cash equivalent assets and liabilities. Each portfolio may contain as many as 100 securities, 20 metals, and 40 other items. In the account transactions section, you enter various account transactions into a master file. These accounts are then posted to the portfolios you've designated.

The securities information section allows you to enter data on all the securities to be analyzed in the portfolio and the accounts sections of the program. This information may be entered manually or automatically through Dow Jones News/ Retrieval. Once you've entered data into the three databases, *Net Worth* may be used to print various types of reports on each portfolio. The program can include information on up to ten items on each report; including asset summary, annualized income, cash dividend summary, interest summary, and list of active buy and sell orders. Each of these reports is prepared on an end-of-the-week basis unless a longer period is specified.

Figure 6-5. Net Worth

	Fair	Good	Very Good	Excellent
Ease of Use	☐	☐	☑	☐
Documentation	☐	☐	☑	☐
Reliability	☐	☑	☐	☐
Cost-effectiveness	☐	☐	☐	☑

Comments: *Net Worth* is a flexible program for maintaining stock portfolio records and for preparing reports on these portfolios. Unlike some other investment software packages, *Net Worth* provides no fundamental or technical analysis along with its record keeping functions, but it does allow you to automatically update stock price information through Dow Jones News/Retrieval. One disadvantage of the program is that it's designed to prepare reports primarily on a weekly or annual basis. It's possible to store information and print reports on a daily basis, but this requires careful setting of the report dates and is awkward. In addition, only 52 weekly (or daily) entries for each security are stored by the program.

Net Worth operates through a system of inter-connected function menus, each of which is initially accessed through the main menu. The *Net Worth* manual is fairly detailed in describing the operation of the program, but it's not well-organized. The manual includes a map of the program menus and an index. No quick reference card is provided.

This program isn't capable of trapping all errors or blocking spurious entries. On two occassions, errors in the program caused it to crash, returning the user to DOS.

The main attraction of *Net Worth* is its excellent report building features. You can generate reports on items such as capital gain/loss, dividends received, and interest earned. Special features include automatic security splitting adjustments for portfolio-owned stocks, setting of high and low sell targets, and computation of reward-to-risk ratios based on latest trading data.

The program can accommodate a variable capital gains holding period to take advantage of the new income tax laws.

Also, when posting a transaction for the acquisition of a security, such as recording the purchase of common stock or securities received as dividend distributions, you may specify the capital gains holding period in months. The default value is six months, though you may change this.

Figure 6-6. *Net Worth* Report

```
               DATA FOR FOLLOWED SECURITIES
                       09/09/83


APPLE COMPUTER        SYMBOL: AAPL    EXCHANGE: OTC    CLOSING PRICE:  30.50
   RECORD NUMBER:  1
   RECENT HIGH: 62.625  LOW: 29.25   TIMELINESS: 3 SAFETY: 2 INT/DIV RATE:

WE   09/09    09/02    08/26     08/19     08/12    08/05    07/29     07/22     07/15
H   39.375   37.875    33.5    33.875    34.25    34.75    43.125    44        47.5
L   30.5     31.25     30.25   33        33.375   33.125   34        41.125    44.125
C   30.5     37.875    30.75   33.625    33.375,  33.875   34.875    43.75     44.125
V   48495    41069     25679   21358     24731    39351    50736     44262     20535



               CAPITAL GAINS/LOSS SUMMARY FOR CY 83
                       09/09/83


MANOR CARE                        NUMBER SOLD:     142.00
   DATE ACQUIRED: 07/29/1976      BASIS PRICE:       2.07
   DATE SOLD: 01/24/1983          SELLING PRICE:    32.00
   NET RETURN:     4514.47        GROSS COST:      313.25
        TERM: LONG                % GAIN/LOSS:    1341.19     GAIN/LOSS:    4201.22
```

Two sample reports showing the value of Apple Computer, Inc. holding (top), and the capital gain for Manor Care (bottom).

The Quick Security Status selection lets you quickly check on holdings for a designated account. The display is sent to the screen and provides similar information as Portfolio Reports Item Data for Owned Securities. The status of the security holdings is based on the latest closing prices available in the security database.

In addition to printed reports, *Net Worth* provides a screen display of up to one year of weekly trading data for any stocks, bonds, precious metals, or stock exchange indexes stored in the database. Take a look at figure 6-6 for a sample report.

Nibble Investor
Company: Nibble Microspark
Computer: Apple II series
Price: $30
Summary: This package is designed to retain your investment portfolio, catalog purchases and sale of each investment, and present (also graphically) the performance of each investment with respect to yield and short- and long-term gain. The program can also analyze sales and market trends through weekly volume tracking and market activity update summaries.

Figure 6-7. Nibble Investor

	Fair	Good	Very Good	Excellent
Ease of Use	☐	☐	☑	☐
Documentation	☐	☑	☐	☐
Reliability	☐	☐	☐	☑
Cost-effectiveness	☐	☐	☑	☐

Comments: Each investment added needs its own file, transactions being written to their corresponding investment files. This approach may appear extravagant with regard to disk space, but there are good reasons for it. This method allows rapid and nondisruptive editing and deletion of whole investments, and since each investment is isolated, the number of transactions for a given investment is limited only by available disk space. Because reports then operate only on entire files, no data parsing is necessary and the program runs faster overall.

Nibble Investor is menu-driven, relatively easy to use, and conceptually straightforward. Although the documentation tends to be sparse, the graphics are very good for a package of this size and accurately represent the information you need to conduct portfolio analysis.

This program helps with the tracking of your portfolio, charting the price/volume movement, and calculating the price/market strength of your investments. It's useful at tax time to assemble the brokerage tickets, reconstruct the purchase information, and calculate the short- and long-term capital gains.

And what about yields? If you're concentrating on income from your portfolio, the dividend yield on individual stocks (and the overall portfolio) is of prime interest. *Nibble Investor* presents this information as well.

Permanent Portfolio Analyzer
Company: C.R. Hunter and Associates, Inc.
Computers: Apple II series, Apple III, IBM PC, IBM PC XT, IBM PC AT, IBM PC-compatibles
Price: $295
Summary: The *Permanent Portfolio Analyzer* stores and organizes an investment portfolio into a set of predefined categories such as gold bullion, stocks, long-term debt, and so on. By retaining the original purchase price and the current price of each investment, this package is able to show how well the portfolio has performed overall in each category. The *Permanent Portfolio Analyzer* also projects the portfolio's future performance based upon a variety of anticipated inflation scenarios.

Figure 6-8. *Permanent Portfolio Analyzer*

	Fair	Good	Very Good	Excellent
Ease of Use	☐	☐	☑	☐
Documentation	☐	☐	☐	☑
Reliability	☐	☐	☐	☑
Cost-effectiveness	☐	☑	☐	☐

Comments: The *Permanent Portfolio Analyzer*'s main strength lies in its ability to summarize your portfolio. Its primary weakness is that it attempts to make projections of what the portfolio will be worth in the future. These ten-year forecasts are based on a user-alterable set of assumptions concerning inflation, future investment prices, and the optimal investment strategy. Given that the true values for these assumptions are difficult, if not impossible, to estimate, the results may be suspect. Clearly, other investment tools, in addition to this package, should also be consulted. The proposed strategy is based on Harry Browne's approach presented in his book *Inflation Proofing Your Investment* (Warner, 1982). This strategy, developed in response to the high inflation of the late 1970s, may not fit the conditions of the next five years.

The program is based on a method for analyzing a long-term investment portfolio in terms of its purchasing power values. After you enter your portfolio, the program produces a balance sheet, which shows current net worth and unrealized gains/losses; and a ten-year projection analysis, which makes projections of portfolio purchasing power in a variety of inflation scenarios. You can easily change the assumptions of this model rather than using Browne's default settings.

Finally, by not marking the date of each investiture, recent and past investments are compared on the same level. Such comparisons may be misleading even to the experienced investor.

Permanent Portfolio Analyzer is an interesting approach to building a set of scenarios or alternatives in order to examine future projections based on an established set of assumptions. Eventually, you'll develop your own set of expectations and a strategy for managing your portfolio.

Personal Investor
Company: PBL Corporation
Computers: Apple II series, IBM PC
Price: $145 (Apple), $195 (IBM)
Summary: The program is an integrated stock information retrieval system designed to connect to an electronic database such as Dow Jones and serve as a portfolio manager. Its primary function as a data retrieval program is described in Chapter 4.

The *Personal Investor* lets you create and manage a portfolio of common stocks, options, bonds, mutual funds, and treasury issues. You can update the portfolio from the Dow Jones News/Retrieval database. *Personal Investor* allows you to store one portfolio per disk. Entering stock data into the record format goes very smoothly. It allows fast, accurate data entry, easy retrieval of stock records, and concise reporting.

Report preparation is simple. Choose the portfolio manager option and select the stock reports option. The program is simple to use and report preparation is straightforward. The program's error handling is very good—it tries to defeat every attempt to enter the wrong data.

Reports can be generated for gains and losses, tax computations, dividends, and price reviews. As an integrated portfolio manager and communication program to connect to Dow Jones or other services, *Personal Investor* is a well-proven winner.

Plain Vanilla
Company: Iris Communications, Inc.
Computers: Apple II series, IBM PC, IBM PC XT, IBM PC AT, IBM PC-compatibles
Price: *The Investor*—$100; *The Manager*—$130; *The Professional*—$160
Summary: The *Plain Vanilla* stock portfolio system consists of three programs—you can decide which to use depending on the sophistication you need. All three use onscreen instructions to guide you through maintaining your portfolio.

The Investor handles 50 securities with up to 50 transactions per security. It provides profit and loss reports and
regular printed reports.

The Manager has the same basic items of *The Investor*,
with the added ability to handle covered call options and up
to ten portfolios, for a total of 100 securities on one disk.

The Professional contains all that's in *The Investor* and *The
Manager*, as well as the ability to do calculations on dividends,
call options, and stock splits. It can also access quotes using
automatic online retrieval from a service such as Dow Jones. It
incorporates the most recent tax laws and permits you to calculate profit and loss including the effects of capital gains.

Portfolio Decisions

Company: Eagle Software Publishing, Inc.
Computer: IBM PC (128K)
Price: $250
Summary: *Portfolio Decisions* provides an investor with a
record keeping function for security transactions from pur-
chases to sales to dividend decisions.

The purchase data is typed into an index card format for
each security. *Decisions* can communicate with a database such
as Dow Jones for entering data. It also provides several reports
for tax decisions.

The program can generate eight different reports. There's
a Portfolio Activity Report that details any transaction in an
investor's stocks, bonds, or other securities such as treasury
bills, mutual funds, options, warrants, or certificates of deposit.
You set the starting and ending date of this report and any
activity is duly noted. The Portfolio Summary Report provides
a quick and easy way to look at the entire portfolio's financial
performance. Of course, there are reports which provide updates on transactions involving individual securities.

The Tickler Report is a simple way to call up pending
activity, such as upcoming dividend dates or options expiration dates. Three tax-reporting forms are available: Interest,
Dividend, and Capital Gains/Losses.

Portfolio Master

Company: Investors Software
Computer: Apple II (64K)
Price: $195

Summary: *Portfolio Master* is a well-developed program for investment portfolio analysis and performance evaluation. It allows you to store information on numerous investment portfolios, to record transactions in the securities found in those portfolios, and to prepare reports on the performance of each portfolio. The menu-driven program records information on nearly every major kind of investment, including common and preferred stock, options, rights, warrants, bonds, and cash.

Current prices and other information for each security may be entered manually or updated automatically using Dow Jones News/Retrieval. Selections from the main menu offer such things as Update Menu, Enter/Delete Menu, Input from Disk, Dow Price Update, Save Portfolio, and Exit.

The Display/Print option lets you analyze the information in each portfolio. Using this, you can list the holdings in each portfolio, prepare a profit and loss statement on each, prepare a report on all transactions, and describe the securities in each portfolio. You may also include notes such as the broker's name or type of investment after the symbol for each security listed.

Figure 6-9. *Portfolio Master*

	Fair	Good	Very Good	Excellent
Ease of Use	☐	☐	☐	☑
Documentation	☐	☐	☐	☑
Reliability	☐	☐	☑	☐
Cost-effectiveness	☐	☐	☐	☑

Comments: *Portfolio Master* is an efficient investment data management program, and should prove useful to most amateur investors and to many professionals as well. The menu system is well-designed and makes the program easy to use. Screen prompts and other user instructions enhance the package.

The reports prepared by this program are also well-designed and easy to read. *Portfolio Master*, however, may occasionally drop you out of the program and into the operating system. The instruction manual lists a procedure to return to the last menu, but this is still annoying. The complete package includes a well-organized instruction manual and a program disk. The manual gives you detailed directions on program startup and operation, as well as instructions on retrieving data from Dow Jones News/Retrieval.

Portfolio Master always lists the components of a portfolio in the following order: common stock, preferred stock, calls, puts, rights, warrants, short sales, bonds, T-bills, and cash. Within each security type, the holdings are arranged in alphabetical order. If you've made multiple purchases of the same security, they're displayed in order of purchase, the most recent listed first.

Figure 6-10. *Portfolio Master* Model Account

```
                            MODEL ACCOUNT

                       PORTFOLIO PROFIT & LOSS
                       AS OF OCTOBER 4, 1984
                                                                  PAGE 1
                                      09/30/1984      GAIN OR LOSS
                     BASIS            ----------------  -------------    %
# UNITS    NAME      DATE     BASIS   PRICE   AMOUNT    SHORT   LONG   CHG
----------------------------------------------------------------------------
   200     ASA       08/15/82  28.89   58.13   11625           5847  101.2
   100     AVP       06/21/81  19.88   32.63    3263           1275   64.1
   100     IBM       09/23/82  70.00  102.75   10275           3275   46.8
   100     IBM       10/10/82  80.00  102.75   10275           2275   28.4
   100     IBM       11/22/83  90.00  102.75   10275.          1275   14.2
   100     IBM       07/22/84 100.00  102.75   10275    1275    275    2.8
   100     WDEPY     12/12/83  29.26   48.75    4875    1949          66.6
   100.1229 KSFOX F  12/01/81   4.55    7.92     793            337   73.9
     1.234 KSFOX F   03/01/82   4.37    7.92      10              4   81.2
     3.336 KSFOX F   06/01/82   4.92    7.92      26             10   61.0
   100     PPLB      03/03/81  81.26   81.26    3700          -4426  -54.5
    10   C HMJD      06/22/84   3.75    7.63    7625    3873         103.2
    10   P EKPO   W  08/08/84   2.26    6.25   -6250   -3985        -159.4
   500   R TRTS   X  07/23/84   0.00    2.38    1188    1188           INF
  1000   W PLTWN  X  08/10/80    .25   55.00   55000          54750  >21M
   200   S XON      02/04/84  41.71   30.00    2343    2010          23.2
    10   M BLHU   T  07/16/81  58.24   78.41    7841           2017   34.6
    10   M T.Z      01/22/82  57.89   81.00    8100           2311   39.9
$10000     BANK #1                            10000
$2000      BANK #2                             2000
 12000     CAPPRES                            12000
   100.25  CAPPRES                              100
   234.4499 CAPPRES                             234
$11000     CERTDEP  (MATURES: 10/23/84)       11000
$13000     FORDPAP  (MATURES: 11/15/84)       12555
$25000     T-BILL   (MATURES: 02/04/85)       23785

           CASH........................$      11000

           TOTAL PORTFOLIO COST..............$  148849
           TOTAL PORTFOLIO VALUE.............$  223912                   49.9

           NET UNREALIZED SHORT TERM GAIN.............$    6585
           NET UNREALIZED LONG TERM GAIN.....................$   67675
           TOTAL NET UNREALIZED GAIN.................................$   74260
----------------------------------------------------------------------------
```

Total profits and losses are illustrated by this *Portfolio Master* report.

The program can handle stock splits and stock dividends. After you enter the required information, the software automatically adjusts the number of shares, the cost price, and the current value. This module also handles splits for calls, puts, rights, and warrants. You can delete the entire sales table at the end of a year and start a new one, a great help when it comes time to report your taxes.

Purchases may be added to the portfolio at any time. When a sale is made, pertinent information can be stored in a sales table. The sales table maintains a record of the long- or short-term, the maturity date of each bond and expiration dates of puts, calls, rights, and warrants.

Documentation is very useful and satisfactorily explains the package's functions. The model portfolio clearly demonstrates *Portfolio Master*'s features.

Reveal

Company: Reveal Software, Inc.
Computers: IBM PC, IBM PC XT, IBM PC AT, IBM PC-compatibles (all require 256K)
Price: $1,550
Summary: *Reveal* is a sophisticated securities and portfolio management system designed for stock brokers and portfolio managers. It records all the securities held in a client's portfolio and all the necessary data related to transactions in those securities, including date, amount, price, symbol of the security, unit commission and fees, and total commission and fees. The program also records important personal and financial information for each current client and prospective client, and can prepare specialized reports according to client name, account, suitability criteria, or specific type of investment. A calendar function for keeping track of appointments, dates, and maturities of securities is also provided. Options are available to update prices automatically through electronic databases, to prepare mailing lists and labels, and to send and receive electronic mail. The automatic price updating is a standard feature of the program. The electronic mail function requires additional system software provided by Reveal Software, Inc., as well as additional hardware for $490, including a modem.

Reveal is menu-prompted, operating through a three-menu system. Up to 4000 client accounts may be stored on a single disk, and as many disks as desired may be used with the system.

Figure 6-11. *Reveal*

	Fair	Good	Very Good	Excellent
Ease of Use	☐	☐	☐	☑
Documentation	☐	☐	☑	☐
Reliability	☐	☐	☑	☐
Cost-effectiveness	☐	☐	☑	☐

Comments: *Reveal* is a very efficient portfolio management program. The menu system is well-organized and easy to follow and, with little practice, it's easy to move quickly from one option to the next. The program provides detailed directions on the screen and leads you through the operation of each function. Program response time is fairly good, both within a given menu function and when moving between menus.

Reveal comes with a complete user's guide which includes an excellent discussion of the menu system and tutorial sections on each major option. The amount of background and reference material available on each function is limited, however. The guide also includes a set of sample reports, and a glossary of financial product symbols and financial terms. No reference card is included.

Stock Folio
Company: Micro Program Designs
Computer: Apple II series
Price: $79.50
Summary: *Stock Folio* (formerly called *Stock Watch*) enables an investor to monitor his or her portfolio transactions and maintain records of closed-out positions. It monitors high, low, close, and volume data for up to 48 securities. The securities' data is manually entered and provisions for a modem and

automatic entry are not provided. The program also offers charts for periods up to 650 days (five years). It will calculate moving averages and plot them with the stock chart. Totally integrated, the package will calculate relative strength and momentum of stock price changes.

Also included is the summary of closed-out positions, an excellent feature which gives you all the IRS Form 1040 Schedule D data needed for filing capital gains and losses on your tax returns.

The program allows for short sales and also provides the means for automatically adjusting any portfolio holding for a stock split or stock dividend.

Its low price makes this program an excellent candidate for the investor with a modest number of stocks that can be tracked by entering data manually.

Stock Portfolio System
Company: Smith Micro Software
Computers: Apple II series, Apple III, Apple Macintosh (512K), IBM PC (192K), IBM PC XT, IBM PC AT, IBM PC-compatibles
Price: $185 (Apple), $225 (Macintosh, IBM PC)
Summary: The *Stock Portfolio System* is a portfolio accounting, record keeping, and timing control system. It was designed for both the personal investor and the stock market professional.

Stock Portfolio System can handle negotiable securities (stocks, options, bonds) and cash type investments (money market, bank account). In essence, *Stock Portfolio System* can handle almost any type of investment that may make up a portfolio.

The program provides two methods of connecting to Dow Jones. In the auto-fetch mode you're connected to Dow Jones and quotes are automatically retrieved for the securities in your portfolio. With the second method, *Stock Portfolio System* turns your computer into a terminal connected to the database. This mode allows you to access *all* the services provided by Dow Jones, such as news, sports, weather, and even its online encyclopedia. Both methods are called by a single keystroke. *Stock Portfolio System* also allows you to enter all your security quotes manually. This is a very simple process; you're prompted all the way.

The program generates up to nine reports, including current portfolio status, profit and loss, interest and dividend income, and expense reports. Up to three margin accounts can be maintained. Figure 6-12 illustrates a current portfolio status report produced by the *Stock Portfolio System*.

Figure 6-12. Portfolio Status

```
                        CURRENT PORTFOLIO STATUS
                          FOR J. Q. INVESTOR
                          AS OF 08/27/83

PURCH INVEST       SECURITY      NO. OF PURCHASE   CURRENT  GAIN/LOSS PERCENT
TYPE  TERM          NAME         SHARES PRICE/SHR PRICE/SHR  PER SHR  CHANGE
----------------------------------------------------------------------------

  C   LONG   APPLE COMPUTER        300    15.75    30.75     15.00     95%
  C   LONG   INT'L BUS MACHINE     200    78.13   117.88     39.75     50%
  M   SHORT  *RCA CORPORATION      200    22.75    26.75      4.00     17%
  O   SHORT  ROCKWELL      NOV 30  500     2.75     1.06     -1.69    -61%
  B   SHORT  XEROX    15.5% 1991     5    89.75   112.50     22.75     25%
  F   SHORT  MASS CO INDEP         200    15.00    13.67     -1.33     -8%


-----------------------MARGIN ACCOUNT DATA-----------------------
        ACCOUNT % REQ      EQUITY $    % EQUITY    PURCHASING POWER
             50           3007.65       65.58           1429.10
             30              0.00        0.00              0.00
             25              0.00        0.00              0.00


----------------------------SUMMARY DATA----------------------------
        PORTFOLIO PURCHASE VALUE                  33762.50
        PORTFOLIO CURRENT VALUE                   47040.25
        TOTAL UNREALIZED GAIN/LOSS                13277.75
                                                  ========
        TOTAL UNREALIZED SHORT TERM GAIN/LOSS       827.75
        TOTAL UNREALIZED LONG TERM GAIN/LOSS      12450.00
                                                  ========
        PURCHASE COMMISSIONS                         91.20
        SALES COMMISSIONS AND COSTS                  91.08
                                                  --------
        TOTAL COMMISSIONS & COSTS YEAR-TO-DATE      182.28
                                                  ========
```

Overall, J.Q. Investor's portfolio has done rather well.

Fundamental
Analysis

Fundamental Analysis

The concept of security analysis is based on the opinion that investors are able to form reliable estimates of a stock's future behavior. Security analysis tries to show what to buy by determining what a security *ought* to be worth.

Fundamental analysis is the study of the financial affairs of a business which enables investors to set a value on a company's securities. Fundamental analysis focuses on determining the intrinsic value of the security and rests on the belief that the value of a security is influenced by the performance of its company. The fundamentals uncovered by this approach help identify situations where stock of quality corporations is available at undervalued prices.

The *intrinsic* value of a security is defined as the present value of all net cash flows to be derived from the ownership of the security. The net cash flows consist of the dividends distributed and the selling price of the security at some future time. Of course, expectations and estimates vary for a given stock. However, the analyst tries to establish estimates of dividends and increases in security price based on several variables, such as quality of the firm's management, the industry's environment, the strength of the company's balance sheet, and its product development. These and other factors are used to determine whether a security is under- or overpriced in relation to its intrinsic value.

This value isn't constant and changes as new information becomes available. A security is underpriced only in the opinion of the analyst; it's not underpriced as far as the market is concerned. The analyst's forecast should produce an above-average rate of return if it's accurate, unique, and significantly different from the market's forecast. However, the stock market is said to be *efficient*, in that the market fully reflects the available information. Nevertheless, investors attempt to discover unique insights and information that will enable them to beat the market.

Fundamental stock analysis is the study of a company's basic characteristics represented by its product or service, earnings, dividends, price-to-earnings ratios, book value, profit margin, return on equity, and other measures. Several programs let you process this data. The simplest approach is to use database software. Any competent database program will do for storing and retrieving information. Communications software can access remote databases such as Dow Jones, and download business information and quotes to a printer or disk for permanent storage. This saves a lot of typing and lets you collect up-to-the-minute information about the stock market, specific companies, or business in general.

The goal of fundamental analysis is to screen a set of candidate securities on the basis of fundamental criteria and select the best candidates. For many fundamental analysts, the forecasted earnings per share and price-to-earnings ratio are the key criteria for selecting stocks.

The Computer Assisted Investment Handbook
Company: Programmed Press (New York)
Computers: Apple II series, Commodore 64, CP/M computers, DEC computers, Kaypro, IBM PC, IBM PC XT, IBM PC AT, IBM PCjr, IBM PC-compatibles, MS-DOS-compatibles, TRS-80 Models 1, 3, and 4
Price: $19.95 (book), $100 (program disk)
Summary: *The Computer Assisted Investment Handbook* is a textbook containing a listing of computer programs for 50 common investment calculations. The programs include calculation of an arithmetic mean, calculation of a moving average, simple time series analysis, regression analysis, present value calculations, bond yield calculations, and option valuation. Each short program is listed in BASIC, along with a few words concerning the use of its financial calculation. You type the program into the computer (saving it to disk makes it permanently available), enter the appropriate data, run the program, and obtain an answer. The same 50 financial programs are also available on a disk offered by the publisher. To make calculations using the disk, you start the program, select a calculation from a master menu, enter the appropriate data, and run the program. To make another calculation, you must restart or *boot* the disk and select a second calculation from the menu; it's not possible to select a second program directly after running one.

Figure 7-1. *The Computer Assisted Investment Handbook*

	Fair	Good	Very Good	Excellent
Ease of Use	☑	☐	☐	☐
Documentation	☑	☐	☐	☐
Reliability	☑	☐	☐	☐
Cost-effectiveness	☑	☐	☐	☐

Comments: *The Computer Assisted Investment Handbook* might be useful to the casual investor who wished to make simple financial calculations on a personal computer. The book and program disk provide a fairly easy method for making these calculations. A more sophisticated investor, however, would carry out most of these calculations, and many others, using a programmable calculator or one of the many available financial software packages. *The Investment Handbook* does provide the user with some explanation of the various programs; the program disk, however, is completely without documentation. In addition, some of the calculations provided in the *Handbook* can become fairly complex, such as option valuation, time series, and regression analysis, and anyone unfamiliar with their underlying mathematical and economic assumptions should be cautious in applying them to investment decisions.

Dow Jones Market Microscope
Company: Dow Jones & Company, Inc.
Computers: Apple II series, Apple III, IBM PC
Price: $700
Summary: *Dow Jones Market Microscope* is a sophisticated program for conducting fundamental analysis of stock prices, company information, and other financial data. It's intended for securities analysts, pension fund and portfolio managers, corporate financial officers, and private investors.

Market Microscope allows you to evaluate corporate financial data on approximately 3200 companies in 180 industries, based on a selection of 62 key financial and business indicators. Both the corporate financial data selected by you and the financial indicators used to evaluate this data are provided by the Media General Financial Services, Corporate Earnings Estimator, and Dow Jones Quotes databases of Dow Jones News/Retrieval.

In other words, you must subscribe to Dow Jones News/Retrieval to make full use of *Market Microscope.* Once you've made contact with the appropriate database and retrieved the desired financial data and stock prices (this data is copied onto your data disk), the *Market Microscope* prepares and sorts this information for fundamental investment analysis.

The program provides two specific routines for the analysis of company financial information: the Price Alert Routine and the Screening Routine. Price Alert prints out a report of all the stocks which have reached critical levels for buying or selling. You preselect these price support and resistance levels, which are recorded on the program's disk. Thus, these parameters apply to the information on all the data disks until they're changed. The Screening Routine ranks all the stocks and industry groups found on a data disk, according to the values of up to 16 key financial indicators. Again, the values of these 16 key indicators can be chosen by you, and are stored on each data disk—they apply to all lists of stocks on that disk. You can store up to 20 lists on each disk, and each list may contain as many as 50 stocks or industry groups.

Figure 7-2. Dow Jones Market Microscope

	Fair	Good	Very Good	Excellent
Ease of Use	☐	☐	☐	☑
Documentation	☐	☐	☐	☑
Reliability	☐	☐	☐	☑
Cost-effectiveness	☐	☐	☑	☐

Figure 7-3. *Microscope* Display

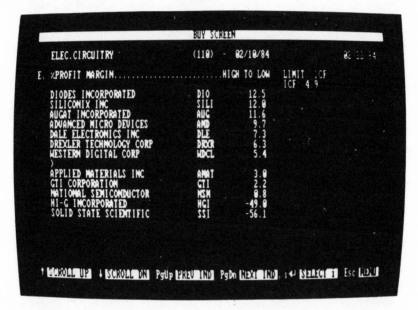

This *Microscope* screen display shows one possible Screening Report.

Comments: *Dow Jones Market Microscope* is very efficient, and though complex, is also fairly easy to use. The program is entirely menu-driven and most commands consist of a single number, letter, or command key. From the main menu, you can select from seven submenus for creating and editing stock lists, screening stocks and industry groups, connecting to Dow Jones, and printing reports and lists of company information.

These submenus are well-organized and the program provides a very good set of screen prompts. The *Market Microscope* comes complete with a system master disk, a backup disk, a data disk, and an instruction manual. The manual provides a tutorial on the use of the program and a section on how to connect to Dow Jones or other databases. It also includes a reference section, list of the available financial indicators, a list of industry group numbers for use in accessing Dow Jones, and a map of the program menus.

Market Microscope is a useful and powerful investment analysis program and should find many users among professional financial analysts and financial officers. Due to the program's price, however, and the cost of continual updates through Dow Jones News/Retrieval, it may not be appropriate for some small, private investors.

The Screening Routine allows you to focus on industry groups that meet your performance requirements, and then screen stocks within those industries to find the best potential investments. You can select up to 20 financial indicators, including Profit Margin, Current Price/Earnings Ratio, Estimated Earnings Per Share, and Return on Total Assets. However, *Microscope* can only screen 50 stocks or industries at a time. The Screening Report organizes and displays the information from the routine; data on stocks and industry groups are ranked and sorted for each indicator. You even select the order for ranking to create a personalized critical limit. Then the Ranking Report provides a concise summary. It numerically ranks stocks according to the selected fundamental indicators and tells you whether or not each stock meets or exceeds the limit you set for the indicator. Figure 7-3 shows a sample display of *Microscope* in action.

Note: *Market Microscope* was recently discontinued by Dow Jones & Company, though you may still be able to find the program for sale in a local computer store, or through software mail order companies.

Evaluation Form, Version 2.0
Company: Investor's Software
Computers: Apple II series, CP/M-based computers, IBM PC
Price: $100
Summary: *Evaluation Form* is a fundamental analysis tool that enables an investor to select stocks for purchase. It utilizes a method of analysis developed by the National Association of Investment Clubs (NAIC). You manually enter data on specific candidate companies, including Standard & Poor's rating, current PE (price/earnings ratio), net profit margins, latest quarter earnings per share, and high and low prices. All of these can be found in financial newspapers as well as in Standard & Poor's handbook.

You'll be able to enter each stock's data in less than 10 minutes. Then the program completes the evaluation calculations and provides a forecast of a high and low price of the candidate stock, a risk/reward ratio, and information on annual yields. *Evaluation Form*'s manual offers a tutorial that effectively explains the calculated data and the underlying method.

Evaluation Form is a very useful aid to the fundamental analysis of common stocks. You can use these techniques to significantly reduce the time necessary to make numerous computations. The result is an effective stock portfolio, preferably one resulting in more profits for you.

Investors Workshop
Company: Dow Jones & Company, Inc.
Computer: Apple II series
Price: $149
Summary: Developed especially for the Apple IIc, but suitable for the entire Apple II series, this program helps you create charts and record the performance of your portfolio.

Figure 7-4. The Screen of Investors Workshop

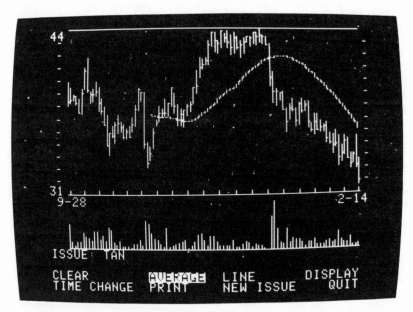

A 19-week moving average charted by *Investors Workshop*.

You can generate charts of moving averages and trend-lines to represent such things as composite daily volume and price action; simple moving averages of closing prices; support or resistance trendlines; or prices and dates of short sales. This package also allows you to maintain a portfolio, generate reports of profits and losses or, using its communications software, access any of the Dow Jones databases.

You're led through a series of prompts as you create a portfolio. The program calculates profit and losses and can update through Dow Jones News/Retrieval. The graphs and reports then can be generated, making this program more than a portfolio manager.

Investors Workshop may be most useful to the investor who relies on fundamental analysis and graphs showing the progress of a stock in the market. This integrated program combines communications, portfolio monitoring, reporting, and graphs, and is compatible with the *Dow Jones Market Analyzer*. *Investors Workshop* has received several rave reviews, and it's worth considering if you need portfolio management, stock charting, and communications in one package.

Invest-Tech
Company: Investment Technologies, Inc.
Price: $250 subscription fee, plus $24 per month minimum, and access charges of $.20 per minute
Summary: An online fundamental analysis program. With a database, you can use it to analyze, screen, chart, find price objectives, project trading ranges, generate timing signals, obtain fundamental rankings, and retrieve data on 4500 stocks, options, and futures.

The screening module, for example, prompts you to set ten factors. If a factor is left blank, the program automatically chooses a default setting. A total of 4500 stocks are then screened—all data is current. The name of each stock which meets your criteria, as well as pertinent information about each, is then printed.

Micro PMS

Company: The Boston Company, Inc.
Computers: Apple II series, Apple III
Price: $495 the first year; $495 each subsequent year for monthly disk updates
Summary: *Micro Portfolio Management System* (PMS) is an investment package consisting of sophisticated investment programs (portfolio accounting, investment analysis, and performance assessment); comprehensive investment data on 1500 stocks, with monthly subscription updates; and authoritative investment advice and counseling. This information has been constructed and arranged to assist you in achieving a clearer understanding of how profitable investment decisions are made.

The package itself is menu-driven, consisting of options allowing you to maintain and analyze your current portfolio. Transactions and up-to-date stock price information are entered so that you can constantly be aware of the portfolio's composition and of new investment opportunities. The program also generates reports which present an analysis of the portfolio's performance over time, its gain, and its yield.

Depending on future investment objectives, whether income, growth, or speculative, the programs offer a set of recommendations regarding various buying and selling strategies. You can select up to 10 criteria from the 50 provided, from growth rate to PE (price/earnings) ratio.

Figure 7-5. *Micro PMS*

	Fair	Good	Very Good	Excellent
Ease of Use	☐	☐	☑	☐
Documentation	☐	☐	☐	☑
Reliability	☐	☐	☐	☑
Cost-effectiveness	☐	☐	☑	☐

Comments: *Micro PMS* is relatively easy to use if you have some experience in stock investment. The documentation guides the experienced user smoothly through each of the package's many functions, supplementing some of the information provided in the program itself.

You can plot any of the information stored on your portfolio as a bar chart or scattergram. Bar charts show different statistics or different investments as a percentage of the total portfolio; scattergrams compare two pieces of information.

For the serious stock investor, *Micro PMS* is recommended as a portfolio management tool. Although the package does offer advice supposedly leading to the "optimal" portfolio, its major advantage lies in how well it systematically organizes and analyzes a portfolio. Obviously, an investment in this package will only pay off for certain individuals, depending upon their degree of knowledge and activity in the stock market.

Considering its price, this program will be most attractive to investors with portfolios exceeding several hundred thousand dollars.

Micro/Scan

Company: Isys Corporation
Computers: Apple II series, Apple III, IBM PC, IBM PC/XT
Price: $6,250 (cash), $12,500 (from your broker after generating so much in commissions [soft money])
Summary: *Micro/Scan* is an advanced program for fundamental investment analysis and portfolio management. Designed primarily for stockbrokers, investment advisors, and sophisticated private investors, *Micro/Scan* provides both an advanced program for conducting fundamental investment analysis and a subscription to the Ford Investor Services Stock database. This database contains 1400 common stocks from the New York, American, and NASDAQ (over-the-counter) exchanges, each evaluated on a series of 54 investment criteria. Stock price, price/earnings ratios, beta value, projected company return on investment (ROI) rate, and company sales are just some of these criteria.

An owner of *Micro/Scan* receives an up-to-date version of this database on disk each month, and can also receive updates more often by calling One/Source, an electronic database network connected to Ford Investor Services. The connection is made through a standard telephone line using an appropriate modem and other equipment. With the program and database, you can then analyze selected portfolios and make investment decisions.

Micro/Scan provides five basic investment analysis capabilities. You can screen the database for selected stocks; prepare reports on an industry, a portfolio, or a single firm; prepare and maintain portfolios; edit the database; and order automatic database updates from One/Source. You're not even limited to the 1400 stocks listed on the Ford Investor Services database. With the database editor, you may add up to 100 nonlisted stocks. In addition, *Micro/Scan* lets you format the database information so that you can use it in a spreadsheet program, such as *VisiCalc* or *Lotus 1-2-3*.

Figure 7-6. *Micro/Scan*

	Fair	Good	Very Good	Excellent
Ease of Use	☐	☐	☑	☐
Documentation	☐	☐	☐	☑
Reliability	☐	☐	☐	☑
Cost-effectiveness	☐	☐	☑	☐

Comments: *Micro/Scan* is a versatile and powerful fundamental investment analysis program. It provides the investor with most of the important financial software functions in a single program, including database management, portfolio management, fundamental analysis, and report preparation. You'll need a few hours of practice to master its numerous features. This program isn't intended for the casual investor, however, due to its complexity, and especially its price. It's definitely aimed at the professional investor.

Micro/Scan is fully menu-prompted, with one main menu and several submenus. You can move from one step to the next, or return to the main menu simply by typing Q (Quit). Nearly all the program commands consist of single numbers, letters, or command keys.

The *Micro/Scan* package includes a master program disk, a database disk, and an instruction manual. The instruction manual includes numerous sample screen displays and report formats, and leads you through each step of the program.

Stockcal
Company: RLJ Software Applications
Computers: IBM PC (64K, one disk drive), IBM PC XT
Price: $40
Summary: *Stockcal* is a common stock investment program designed to conduct the calculations involved in the "Stock Selection Guide" used in many personal investment clubs.

The Stock Selection Guide is a method of common stock investment analysis recommended to investment clubs by the National Association of Investment Clubs. It's assumed that users of *Stockcal* also own the *Investor's Manual* for instructions on how to store and update information on companies issuing common stock, as well update stock price, volume, and dividend data.

Figure 7-7. *Stockcal*

	Fair	Good	Very Good	Excellent
Ease of Use	☐	☐	☑	☐
Documentation	☐	☐	☑	☐
Reliability	☐	☐	☑	☐
Cost-effectiveness	☐	☐	☐	☑

Stockcal stores the company name, number of shares, long term debt, and annual and quarterly sales and earnings information. The program then assembles this information and calculates projected five-year earnings and stock price estimates, based on a user-defined growth rate or estimated stock price.

Figure 7-8. IBM Projected Sales and Earnings (1984-1988)

```
IBM(N)                    9/28/84   610.7 M Sh                    SALES    E P S
:   :   :   :   :   :   :   :   :   :   1   :   :   :   :   :         YEAR      MIL $    IN $
:   :   :   :   :   :   :   :   :   :   1   :   :   :   :   E         ====      =====    =====
:   :   :   :   :   :   :   :   :   :   1   :   E   E   E   :         1974     12675.0    3.12
:   :   :   :   :   :   :   :   :   :   E   E   :   :   :   :         1975     14437.0    3.34
:   :   :   :   :   :   E   :   E   1   :   :   :   :   :   S         1976     16304.0    3.99
:   :   :   :   E   E   :   E   :   1   :   S   S   S   :   :         1977     18133.0    4.58
:   :   E   E   :   :   :   :   :   S   S   :   :   :   :   :         1978     21076.0    5.32
E   E   :   :   :   :   :   S   S   1   :   :   :   :   :   :         1979     22863.0    5.16
:   :   :   :   :   S   S   :   1   :   :   :   :   :   :   :         1980     26213.0    6.10
:   :   S   S   S   :   :   :   1   :   :   :   :   :   :   :         1981     29070.0    5.63
S   S   :   :   :   :   :   :   1   :   :   :   :   :   :   :         1982     34364.0    7.39
:   :   :   :   :   :   :   :   1   :   :   :   :   :   :   :         1983     40180.0    9.04
:   :   :   :   :   :   :   :   1   :   :   :   :   :   :   :    Hist. S G =13.3%  Hist. E G =11.3%
:   :   :   :   :   :   :   :   1   :   :   :   :   :   :   :    Est. FSG? 12      Est. FEPSG? 12
:   :   :   :   :   :   :   :   1   :   :   :   :   :   :   :         1984     43274.7    9.26
:   :   :   :   :   :   :   :   1   :   :   :   :   :   :   :         1985     48467.6   10.37
:   :   :   :   :   :   :   :   1   :   :   :   :   :   :   :         1986     54283.7   11.61
:   :   :   :   :   :   :   :   1   :   :   :   :   :   :   :         1987     60797.8   13.01
:   :   :   :   :   :   :   :   1   :   :   :   :   :   :   :         1988     68093.5   14.57
:   :   :   :   :   :   :   :   :   1   :   :   :   :   :   :
-------------------------------------------------------
1   2   3   4   5   6   7   8   9   10  11  12  13  14  15
Long term debt (in millions) =$2674.0
```

```
% Pre-tax profit on sales: 24.3 22.5 20.6 23.1 23.6    ave = 22.8    NO TREND
% Earned on invs. capital: 20.1 21.6 18.4 22.3 23.8    ave = 21.2    NO TREND

Present price =105.25        High this year=134.25        Low this year= 99.00

YEAR    HIGH    LOW      EPS      HIGH PE     LOW PE      DIV     % PO     % HY
1979    80.50   61.13    5.16     15.6        11.8        3.44    66.7     5.6
1980    72.75   50.38    6.10     11.9        8.3         3.44    56.4     6.8
1981    71.50   48.38    5.63     12.7        8.6         3.44    61.1     7.1
1982    98.00   55.63    7.39     13.3        7.5         3.44    46.5     6.2
1983   134.25   92.25    9.04     14.9        10.2        3.71    41.0     4.0
Ave low price=61.55      Ave high PE=13.7      Ave low PE= 9.3    Ave % payout 54.4
Average price earnings ratio =11.5            Current price earnings ratio=10.7

Projected high price=199.13 assuming a 12 % growth rate

Low prices: (ave low PE)(curr erns)= 83.95    Select estimated low price? 70
            Ave low for last 5 years= 61.55
            Recent severe market low= 48.38    ZONES: LOWER    70.00 to 113.04
            Price div.  will support= 53.44           MIDDLE  113.04 to 156.09
Up-Down Ratio= 2.66                                   UPPER   156.09 to 199.13
Present yield 3.61
Ave yld over next 5 yrs  6.08

Last years quarterly sales:  8287.0    9590.0    9410.0   12900.0
This years quarterly sales:  9585.0   11199.0    N AV      N AV

% quarterly sales increase:  15.66     16.78     N M       N M

Last years quarterly earns:   1.62      2.22      2.14      3.06
This years quarterly earns:   1.97      2.65      N AV      N AV

% quarterly earns increase:  21.60     19.37     N M       N M
```

A wide variety of information appears in *Stockcal*'s printed reports, including projected high price (199.13) and average yield over the next five years (6.08).

You can vary these estimates and recalculate the price and earnings projections, seeing as many as you want before making an investment decision. *Stockcal* prints out the company information and price and earnings projections in a format specified by the Stock Selection Guide. Menu-driven, with a single main menu, the program saves and edits company information on disk files.

Comments: *Stockcal* is a straightforward common stock investment analysis program. The main menu and screen instructions are easy to follow and program response time is very good. The process of entering data and running the program, however, may be confusing to some. All company and stock price data is entered on the IBM PC in DATA statements before RUN is typed to reenter and start the program, and save the information. Program documentation is not very detailed or complete, consisting only of six to eight loose-leaf pages. *Stockcal* is intended primarily for people belonging to investment clubs; it should be adequate for their needs. Other investors should consider purchasing a more general investment analysis program, such as *Evaluation Form*. Figure 7-8 illustrates the kind of printed reports you can expect from *Stockcal*.

Stockpak II
Company: Standard & Poor's Corporation
Computer: Apple II series
Price: $245 (for each database and program), $490 OTC
Summary: *Stockpak II* is a sophisticated program for fundamental stock analysis and screening. The program lets you screen stocks in one of four databases, look up data on any listed stock, compare stock performance graphically, and prepare reports on any stocks in the database. The four databases include a New York Stock Exchange (NYSE) database of 1500 stocks, an American Stock Exchange (AME) database of 800 stocks, an over-the-counter (OTC) database of 2200 stocks, and a composite database of 1500 stocks.

The information in these databases is not available online, but instead is supplied on disks. You can subscribe to any of the four databases—disk updates are sent to you monthly.

Stock screening and look-up features let you compare companies based on 100 different investment criteria. These criteria include price, trading volume, dividend yield, beta, industry group, Standard & Poor's rank, and earnings-per-share growth. The program provides you with three preselected sets (ten criteria each) for stock screening. Of course, you can create your own criteria sets. The screening routine is fairly quick, and takes about 30 seconds for one screening using a ten-item criteria set. *Stockpak II* includes a data integrity card which allows you to customize the program and to make backup copies of the data disks.

Figure 7-9. *Stockpak II*

	Fair	Good	Very Good	Excellent
Ease of Use	☐	☐	☐	☑
Documentation	☐	☐	☑	☐
Reliability	☐	☐	☐	☑
Cost-effectiveness	☐	☐	☑	☐

Comments: *Stockpak II* is well-designed and allows you to quickly scan a large number of companies and common stocks according to key criteria and then to conduct a more thorough analysis. The lack of online updating shouldn't be a hindrance to most investors, since new disks are provided monthly. However, if you're an investor who trades daily or weekly, and want *instant* price updates, you should think about using another software package.

Stockpak II is menu-prompted, with the main menu offering six options, including looking up company information, comparing information on several companies, screening a database, preparing a report, accessing support functions, and exiting. The package includes a single program disk, data disks for each ordered database, and a complete instruction manual.

If you want to look up information on a specific company, choose item 1 from the main menu and you'll be prompted for the official ticker symbol. The search only takes about five seconds, and the information is displayed on three screen pages.

Or you can use the Screen feature and have the program search for all the stocks in a database which meet your requirements. Unfortunately, Screen only lists the ticker symbols of companies—not names. Unless you follow the stock market closely, chances are you don't have ticker symbols and their corresponding companies memorized.

Besides the normal information about how to get the software up and running, the manual contains definitions of financial terminology. The manual is quite good, with plenty of screen illustrations. Strangely enough, there are no page numbers or index.

Telescan
Company: Telescan, Inc.
Computer: IBM PC (256K), IBM PC XT, IBM PC AT, IBM PCjr, IBM PC-compatibles
Price: $395
Summary: A fundamental analysis program using a database of up to 6500 stocks for a period of one month to ten years. You can determine insider selling, dividends, cash flow, book value, and capital spending for a company. Excellent charts are formatted for viewing and printout.

Value/Screen
Company: Value Line, Inc.
Computers: Apple II series, IBM PC, IBM PC XT
Price: $443 per year for monthly disk updates (trial subscription of $39 for two months); $211 per year for quarterly disk updates
Summary: *Value/Screen* is a fundamental investment analysis program exclusively for use with the common stock investment data compiled by Value Line, Inc. The package includes two computer disks: a master disk which contains *Value/Screen*, and a data disk containing the current investment data for each of the 1650 common stocks listed and evaluated in the Value Line Investment Survey. Prior to *Value/Screen*, the Value Line Investment Survey data was only available by mail subscription or in local libraries. Now this information may be obtained on disk and evaluated with a personal computer.

Value/Screen is organized around a single master menu with options such as Begin Screening, Add Parameter, Report on Stocks Selected, Report on Specific Stock, and conduct

Statistical Analysis of Stocks Selected. Each stock on the *Value/Screen* data disk is evaluated according to 32 investment, dividend, growth rate, and beta values. The proprietary Timeliness Rank and Safety Rank variables reported in the Value Line Investment Survey are also available.

To begin an analysis, you select the desired variables and the program screens the list and returns results. You can print a report of this listing or conduct a statistical analysis of each stock. The statistical analysis calculates the mean, variance, standard deviation, range, and sample size of any variable for any stock. If the screened list is larger or smaller than desired, or if it doesn't contain the desired stocks, you can change the variables, their values, and see a new screen.

Figure 7-10. *Value/Screen*

	Fair	Good	Very Good	Excellent
Ease of Use	☐	☐	☑	☐
Documentation	☐	☐	☑	☐
Reliability	☐	☐	☐	☑
Cost-effectiveness	☐	☐	☑	☐

Comments: *Value/Screen* is an efficient and well-organized program for the fundamental analysis of common stocks. It's probably the program of choice for any investor who uses the Value Line Investment Survey as a basis for making investment decisions. The program provides the investor with a complete and up-to-date listing of all the stocks evaluated by Value Line. Each owner of *Value/Screen* receives a new, updated disk every month. Obviously, the program would be less interesting to an investor who wished to study stocks and other securities not evaluated by Value Line.

Including a master program disk, a data disk, and an instruction manual, *Value/Screen*'s documentation is fairly complete, but could be more detailed in describing the program's operation. However, the guide does contain a list of definitions for each of the 32 variables and a complete listing of the stocks included in the Value Line Investment Survey.

Value/Screen will profile any 50 stocks that you request. Each month, the same 50 company profiles will be updated. At the core of the service are Value Line's proprietary measures, which assign a rank to every one of the stocks stored on the disk. These are derived from Value Lines's private database of current and historical securities information. A set of computer models assigns ranks by screening the database according to price/earnings ratios, quarterly earnings, price momentum, and other criteria.

One shortcoming of *Value/Screen* is its inability to change or update the information in the main database. Neither an online nor a manual method exists. As a result, the *Value/Screen* data is most valuable for only a short time. It would certainly be more attractive if you could update important data by hand, and have the program recalculate the affected variables. *Value/Screen*'s greatest strength lies in its ability to let you create and test the performance of several different investment strategies. Of course, the success of any past strategy doesn't mean that it will be equally successful in the future. But, as the manual says, it obviously helps to test a strategy on paper before committing your funds. *Value/Screen* (especially when you take it on a two-month trial basis) offers an inexpensive approach to investment strategy development.

8

Technical Analysis

Technical Analysis

Technical analysis is the study of internal market phenomena, such as patterns of price movement, in an attempt to forecast the future movement of the market or individual investments within the market. Often, technical analysis is used in conjunction with fundamental analysis. Fundamentalists forecast stock prices on the basis of economic, industry, and company statistics, and a stock's earnings and dividends. Technicians, on the other hand, believe the forces of supply and demand are reflected in patterns of price and volume of trading. Moreover, this approach assumes that price fluctuations reflect logical market forces which can be discerned and which can be used to predict future trends. Technical analysis also focuses on timing of decisions, such as when to buy or when to sell.

Indicators to measure the direction of the overall market are used in technical analysis, as well as considerations of the stock and bond market patterns over time. But one of the most valuable tools of the technical analyst is the chart.

History tends to repeat itself—that's the basic premise for using charts. Charts are a form of graphic ticker tape of price and volume combined with a summary of long-term patterns. Primarily regarded as a timing tool, the chart can also be a valuable source of information for stock selection. By comparing charts of individual stocks to those for the major market indices, various combinations of securities can be rapidly screened. Most charts cover a relatively long period of time, enabling the computer user to obtain a considerable amount of historical data from a single source. Of course, charts aren't infallible.

Technical Analysis Methods

One particularly popular method of technical analysis is based on the *Dow theory*, named after Charles H. Dow, one of the founders of the Dow Jones Industrial Average. The Dow approach is used to identify the end of a bull or bear market. It results in an after-the-fact verification of what's already happened. The Dow theory concentrates on the long-term trend in

market behavior (known as the *primary trend*) and largely ig-
nores day-to-day fluctuations or secondary movements. The
Dow Jones Industrial and Transportation Averages are used to
assess the position of the market. Once a primary trend in the
Industrial Average has been established, the market tends to
move in that direction until the trend is canceled out by *both*
the Industrial and Transportation Averages. This is known as
confirmation and happens when secondary movements in the
Industrial Average are confirmed by secondary movements in
the Transportation Average.

Another approach uses the number of *advances and declines* of stocks. A common index is determined by calculating
the daily net difference between the number of New York
Stock Exchange stocks that advance and the number of those
that decline. This net difference is added to the next day's difference, and so on, to form a continuous cumulative index.
The index is plotted in line form and compared with the Dow
Jones Industrial Average. When they diverge, it's assumed that
the advance-decline line will show the true direction of the
market.

Yet another market indicator is the number of *new high
prices* for the year achieved on a given day, less the number of
new lows. The theory is that a rising market will generally be
accompanied by an expanding number of stocks reaching new
highs and a dwindling number of new lows. The reverse holds
true for a declining market. The number of New York Stock
Exchange stocks making new highs for the year, minus the
number making new lows, is averaged for a five-day period. A
moving average smooths out erratic daily fluctuations and
shows the trend. Such a high/low index would normally
move with the market. Divergence from the market trend is a
clue to future price movements.

Obviously, individual investors are free to formulate and
track their own market indicators using their personal computers. The difficulty is that the development of a variable indicator means some significant work. The key question is *Can
the indicator predict a market change,* or *determine if a turn in
the market is a trend or just a temporary transient change?*

Technical analysts have developed hundreds of methods
in trying to identify and project these trends, using data relating to market activity or individual securities. Some techniques

are based on only one or two items of information and fairly simple calculations, like moving averages.

A *moving average* is a mean or average equalling the total set of data, divided by the total number of observations. The moving average is compiled by dropping the oldest data as the newest is added. For instance, if we calculated 5-day and 40-day moving averages of the closing price of a particular security and plotted these on a graph for several weeks, we'd probably see points at which the two lines crossed.

A buy signal is indicated when the average based on the shorter period crosses and rises above the longer period average price. A sell signal is shown when the 5-day average crosses and falls below the 40-day average.

Charts

Thus the wide use of charts in technical analysis. Generally, two kinds of charts are used, the vertical line (bar chart) and the point and figure chart. Although both tell the same story, their preparation is different. *Bar charts* are simple graphic representations of daily (though sometimes weekly or monthly) stock prices—highs, lows, and closing prices. An entry on graph paper is made every trading day, and volume bars are maintained at the bottom.

Point and figure charting is more complicated, since it lacks the dimension of time. On chart paper, Xs, Os, or actual prices are entered if there is a substantial and predetermined change or reversal from the previous price. Prices are vertically plotted, usually in one-half point, one-point, or two-point gradations until there's a change in trend, when the next vertical column is started. There's no volume measurement.

Both kinds of charts are meant to identify the five phases which make up a cycle in the life of a stock movement:

• Accumulation
• Recovery
• Speculation
• Distribution
• Readjustment

Analysis 1
Company: Galaxy
Computer: Apple II series
Price: $70
Summary: *Analysis 1* is a graphics-oriented program designed to analyze the Dow Jones Industrial Average data. The program comes with a historical file of data since 1904. Between six months and five years can be plotted on the screen at any time.

Extensive color graphics are used. From six months to five years of your selected Dow Jones Industrial data can be plotted on the screen in one of five colors with the Apple's high resolution capabilities. The Dow Jones Industrial data can be transformed into differently colored graphic representations called *transforms*. These transforms come in several forms, including your specified moving averages; a least squares linear fit (best straight line); filters for time, magnitude, or percentage changes; and relationships between the data which you specify.

Analyst
Company: K-Wave Financial Services
Computers: CP/M-based computers, IBM PC, IBM PC XT
Price: $1,500 for CP/M based versions; $895 for IBM versions
Summary: *Analyst* is a high-resolution technical analysis graphics program capable of displaying charts. *Analyst* provides for all forms of technical analysis, including bar charts, logarithmic price plots, and price-volume displays. The program also gives you the option to create your own formulas for stock valuation based on high, low, and closing market prices as well as stock volume.

Securities prices can be updated from Dow Jones, CompuServe, and the Bridge financial data retrieval systems.

Brandon Stock System
Company: Brandon Information Management
Computer: IBM PC
Price: $325
Summary: The *Brandon Stock System* is a technical analysis program for tracking stocks, bonds, options, and mutual funds. The program incorporates a proprietary buy/sell analysis formula which recommends nine various actions you can take on a given stock. The manual advises using the buy/sell formula

only with stocks, not with bonds, mutual funds, or options. The program can store and analyze up to one year of price and volume trading data. It features automatic updating of up to 45 stocks from Dow Jones News/Retrieval, and produces video graphics on either color or monochrome displays.

Once you've entered the names of the initial stocks you want to follow, or added a stock to an existing list, the program provides an option to update the recently added stocks through a series of menus either manually or automatically. The analysis technique requires daily price and volume data for all stocks on your list. If you're following a small number of stocks, say ten or less, consider manual updating. For many stocks, current price and volume data are readily available in your daily newspaper. When more than ten stocks are involved, you should start thinking about automatic updating.

As the daily pricing and volume data are entered and passed through the system's buy/sell algorithm, action signals are generated for certain stocks. Only those stocks that are both tracked and whose price and volume history cause the program to recommend an action show up on the action summary report.

The *Brandon Stock System* can recommend nine actions, from Blank (do nothing) or Buy to Sell (Protect With Sell Stop Order) or Fast Sell. You'd be well-advised to use this program on a simulated (no actual purchase) basis for six months before actually using it. Since it has a proprietary algorithm for recommended actions, many investors may find it difficult to use the *Brandon System*. If you're like most technical investors, you like to understand the underlying basis for your decisions.

Compu Trac
Company: The Technical Analysis Group
Computers: Apple II+, IIe (48K), IBM PC (256K)
Price: $1,974, plus $200 annual maintenance fee (Apple); $1,900, plus $300 annual maintenance fee (IBM). A demonstration disk is available for $10 (both versions).
Summary: *Compu Trac* is not a single program, but instead a coordinated group which allows many kinds of technical analysis and mathematical manipulation of commodities and stock prices, and market averages. Among these programs are those for creating bar charts, point and figure charts, momentum indices for both stocks and commodities, and Gann

Cardinal Squares. Other facilities include an oscillator, overbought/oversold index, relative strength index, commodity spread, Fourier analysis, and many more.

One method within the *Compu Trac* system is the Profit Matrix. It can evaluate a variety of systems using whatever data you choose. Your information can be tick prices converted from *Compu Trac's* Intra-day Analyst, daily prices from the regular program, monthly averages, or almost anything in between. You have to be able to specify your system in terms of oscillator-type signals. For each run, you identify a single time series that represents your trading indicator. Profit Matrix can then calculate signals for decisions and test run reports.

Dow Jones Market Analyzer
Company: Dow Jones & Company, Inc.
Computers: Apple II series, Apple III, IBM PC (with color card), IBM PC XT, TI Professional
Price: $350
Summary: The *Dow Jones Market Analyzer* is a highly sophisticated program for the technical analysis of stock prices and other financial data. *Market Analyzer* provides you with nearly all of the most important charting techniques currently used in technical analysis. Several types of moving average charts, straight line charts, indicator charts, and oscillator charts are available to you. The program also offers relative strength and comparison charts. Each of these charts may be drawn alongside the plot of prices for an individual stock, and several may be displayed atop one another to give a detailed picture of a stock's price movement over time. In addition, the data from more than one security may be shown on the same plot, allowing a comparison between two or more stocks, or between a stock and a market index. The program will plot stock prices and charts on either color or monochrome monitors (however, the IBM PC monochrome display is not compatible), and will print any graph with a suitable printer.

In addition to its powerful charting capabilities, the *Market Analyzer* lets you access Dow Jones News/Retrieval and other data services. Data on stock prices and other information may be entered manually, or automatically through Dow Jones when you have a modem. Once the telephone number of the database is typed in, *Market Analyzer* automatically dials it, connects to the service, and writes to disk the new or updated stock prices. After the data is recorded, you simply disconnect and begin the technical analysis. The program stores up to 300 days of stock prices for 33 stocks on a single disk (or 120 days of prices for up to 100 stocks).

Figure 8-1. *Dow Jones Market Analyzer*

	Fair	Good	Very Good	Excellent
Ease of Use	☐	☐	☑	☐
Documentation	☐	☐	☐	☑
Reliability	☐	☐	☐	☑
Cost-effectiveness	☐	☐	☑	☐

Comments: The *Dow Jones Market Analyzer* is not only sophisticated and efficient, but it's also quite easy to use. The program is menu-driven and extremely well-organized. From the main menu you can select separate menus for preparing individual charts and comparison charts, for connecting to Dow Jones News/Retrieval, and for printing charts. The program is also simple to run; it usually requires only single-letter commands to prepare a chart, revise an earlier chart, or move from one menu to another.

The program comes with a system master disk, a working program disk, two data disks, and a reference manual. The latter includes a set of instructions for setting up the system, connecting to a database, and running the technical analyses. It also discusses the use and interpretation of technical charts in stock market analysis, and maps all program commands. *Dow Jones Market Analyzer* is a powerful and cost-effective program that should appeal to many styles of investors.

Restrictions in the Dow Jones News/Retrieval database make the *Market Analyzer* a better tool for short-term than for long-term analysis. Only one year of historical data is available, and only daily price updates are available. That can get cumbersome and expensive for someone who only really needs weekly or monthly numbers.

Market Analyzer plots its charts with a variety of line styles, including horizontal, parallel, and trend lines. These make it easy to distinguish one stock from another in comparison charts. Comparison charts graph high, low, and close for up to five stocks simultaneously, in color. A minor problem is *Market Analyzer*'s inability to recognize stock splits while printing or displaying a chart. If the stock you're analyzing has split within the period you're charting, it shows up on the chart as a disconcerting gap.

Market Analyst
Company: Anidata
Computers: Apple II series, IBM PC
Price: $495
Summary: *Market Analyst* is a menu-driven package designed to help investors manage and analyze their current investments.

Besides evaluating your own holdings, the package may also be used to evaluate other potential investments. The program is made up of three sections: the Portfolio Manager; the Technical Analyst; and News, Views, and Quotes. The first section helps you manage and evaluate your portfolios. For instance, by accumulating relevant stock information, you're able to evaluate each stock, thus maintaining an optimal portfolio.

The second section lets you graphically project the future performance of various stocks. Besides forecasting stock prices, this also provides an excellent way of evaluating the past performance of stocks. The third section accesses remote information services (Warner, CompuServe, and so on) through a modem to receive up-to-date financial information.

Comments: *Market Analyst* is relatively easy to use, assuming you have a substantial understanding of portfolio management and forecasting. If you fit this category, the package is a satisfactory way of organizing and analyzing a portfolio.

One of the package's strengths is its graphics abilities. Representing a stock's price over time gives you a suitable method of determining how well it's performed. The graphics are also very useful for many of the forecasting techniques, even though it's not a good idea to rely on them too heavily.

Figure 8-2. *Market Analyst*

	Fair	Good	Very Good	Excellent
Ease of Use	☐	☐	☑	☐
Documentation	☐	☐	☐	☑
Reliability	☐	☐	☐	☑
Cost-effectiveness	☐	☐	☑	☐

Technical analysis requires manipulating and charting large amounts of data. It's time-consuming and, to be effective, must be done frequently. Computerizing the calculations and charting has helped technical analysts do more in less time, increasing their productivity and presumably the value of their portfolios.

Technical charting ability, together with portfolio accounting and communications for retrieving news, views, and quotes, is a good summary of the computer power a technical analyst can put to use. This combination is an accurate description of the *Market Analyst* package. For instance, the program calculates and displays simple, weighted, and exponential moving averages, and the average of the last line plotted. The system creates moving average trading bands (simple, moving, or exponential).

It also provides volume histograms, positive and negative volume indicators, on-balance volume charts, and accumulation/distribution functions. The program creates trend and support/resistance lines.

The package includes built-in functions for relative strength analysis, generation of relative strength indexes, linear regression, and L. Williams' stochastic calculation. It allows you to specify your own formulas (such as oscillators, volatility analysis, and comparative performance) and to apply them using only two keystrokes. You don't need to understand programming to specify your formulas. This simplicity is one of the package's strengths.

On balance, Anidata's *Market Analyst* is slightly easier to use than *Dow Jones Market Analyzer*. With its user-defined functions and the included portfolio manager, the Anidata product has a slight edge over Dow Jones'.

Market Counselor

Company: Capital Management Systems, Inc.
Computers: Apple II series, IBM PC, IBM PC AT
Price: $195
Summary: *Market Counselor*, a standard technical investment analysis program for use by both professional and private investors, is designed to help evaluate the timing of up or down moves in the overall stock market. It may be used to try to find the best entry point into the market for transactions. The program generates a market indicator based upon six years of market data, which is included with the program. The data analyzed and charted by *Market Counselor* consists of a set of 14 stock market indicators from the New York Stock Exchange (NYSE). This program does *not* chart or analyze data for individual stocks.

Indicators include the date, Dow Jones Industrial Average closing price, total number of advances and declines, total volume, total up volume and down volume, and total odd lot sales and odd lot short sales. Also included are a Relative Strength Index, an Intermediate Index, and an Overbought/Oversold Index.

The *Market Counselor* data disk contains current data and historical data files. The former holds up to 60 days of values for the market indicators, while the latter contains all information older than 60 days, filed by quarter. The past several months of data on each market indicator are included on the data disk when you buy the program; you have to manually enter all subsequent data. *Market Counselor* charts each of the indicators and also prints out these charts. You can then use these charts to determine the likely moves of the stock market, and plan an investment strategy accordingly.

Comments: *Market Counselor* performs one principal function—technical analysis of the overall New York Stock Exchange.

But in addition to its charting features, *Market Counselor* offers a detailed discussion of the use and interpretation of technical stock market indicators. Over two-thirds of the instruction manual is devoted to this. Unlike some other technical analysis programs, however, *Market Counselor* doesn't provide for the analysis or plotting of prices of individual stocks, nor does it offer automatic updating from a database.

Menu-driven, the package includes a program disk, a market indicator data disk, and an instruction manual. The manual is quite detailed, but the instructions aren't always clear. An index, reference section on technical stock market analysis, and an appendix on system setup are part of the manual, though. A Color Graphics Adapter card, or its equivalent, is required to run the program on the IBM computers.

Figure 8-3. *Market Counselor*

	Fair	Good	Very Good	Excellent
Ease of Use	☐	☐	☐	☑
Documentation	☐	☐	☑	☐
Reliability	☐	☐	☐	☑
Cost-effectiveness	☐	☐	☑	☐

All but one of the indicators which *Market Counselor* plots are well-known, established technical indexes. The exception is a proprietary, intermediate index. According to the documentation, this index is "a composite of a large portion of the data entered each time the files are updated. The composite is then smoothed with a moving average." No further explanation is provided. The documentation then gives examples of times in the past when the index has given the correct buy or sell signals, along with instructions on how to interpret the performance of this special index. (You could use this program wihout the proprietary index, since its basis isn't explained.) If you do follow the market timing philosphy, however, you might find it extremely useful. As with other techniques you're unfamiliar with, it's probably a good idea to use it for some time as a simulation, without actually investing your own money.

Market Counselor can track only one quarter (90 days) of information at a time; this limitation will severely affect the analysis of many technicians.

Market Mood Monitor
Company: Computer Asset Management
Computers: Apple II series, IBM PC (192K, color graphics capability, and monitor)
Price: $185
Summary: *Market Mood Monitor* is a standard technical investment program which calculates and charts 24 technical stock market indicators based on a set of 11 pieces of information you enter. It's designed for either the professional or private investor, and can evaluate the timing of up or down movements in the market.

The 24 indicators are grouped into six categories, including advance-decline, new high-lows, volume charts, futures, and short sales. The sixth category (other) includes both the 12-day rate-of-change and a moving average for the New York Stock Exchange (NYSE) composite index, in addition to a trend indicator, trading index, and on-balance volume. Like *Market Counselor*, this program does not chart individual stocks.

The NYSE composite index is plotted below each displayed chart, showing a visual analysis of any indicator-to-market relationship. Charting options allow you to draw your own trendlines, buy and sell arrows, overlay charts, and grids. A pointer arrow can be moved across the chart of either 14 months of daily data or six years of monthly data, while the screen displays each individual date to which the arrow points.

The accompanying data disk contains records of the previous five years. Its information may be updated either manually from what's published in the *Wall Street Journal* or *Barron's*, automatically by modem from Computer Asset Management's online database ($120 per year), or by subscription, with either weekly or monthly shipments of updated disks ($5.25 per week or $12 per month).

Figure 8-4. *Market Mood Monitor*

	Fair	Good	Very Good	Excellent
Ease of Use	☐	☐	☐	☑
Documentation	☐	☐	☑	☐
Reliability	☐	☐	☑	☐
Cost-effectiveness	☐	☐	☑	☐

Figure 8-5. Charting with *Market Mood Monitor*

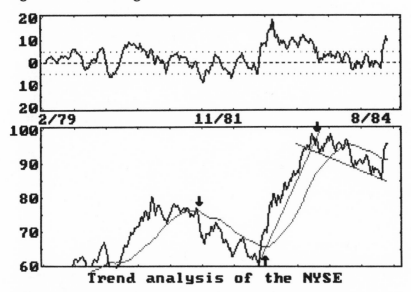

This chart was produced by the IBM PC version of Market Mood Monitor.

Comments: The *Market Mood Monitor* is reliable and, after some getting used to, easy to use. The program is menu-prompted, with fairly self-explanatory displays that make it difficult to create errors. Although the program sets up slowly, once that's done its response time is short. The instruction manual is well-organized and easy to read. It has sections explaining each part of each menu, along with a section on graph interpretation, though (as stated in its introduction) it's assumed that you have some familiarity with this type of technical analysis.

The *Market Mood Monitor* is designed to aid investors in making market timing decisions. Market timing is important for those investors interested in stock index futures, mutual funds, or individual stocks. (Just remember that the program tracks the NYSE market as a whole, not individual stocks.)

Market Mood Monitor doesn't generate buy and sell signals—you must make those decisions yourself. The program will, however, help you make market timing decisions. These decisions can now be based on graphic analysis of overbought/ oversold conditions, market breadth, market momentum, and your own market timing model.

The program includes a Sentiment Indicator that graphically displays investor sentiment, allowing you to buy when the "crowd" is pessimistic (and stocks are underpriced) and sell when the "crowd" is optimistic (and prices are over-valued). By following investor sentiment you can see developing overbought/oversold conditions. The Sentiment Indicator is a composite of all the technical indicators tracked by *Market Mood Monitor*. You can even specify the combination of technical indicators, creating your own Sentiment Indicator!

Market Technician
Company: Datamost, Inc.
Computer: Apple II series
Price: $50
Summary: The *Market Technician* lets you store and plot the stock price and volume data for up to 40 individual stocks. The program stores up to 120 days of price and volume data for each stock. This information may be entered manually or automatically through Dow Jones News/Retrieval. The *Market Technician* also allows you to calculate and plot any of 13 technical market indicators based on a stock market database provided. This market database includes five years of New York Stock Exchange (NYSE) data (January 2, 1979 to the present), including that on trading volume, issues advancing and declining, and the Dow Jones Industrial Average.

Market Technician constructs a data file from any 120-day period within this database, calculates the 13 technical indicators, and plots these indicators on the screen or printer. The 13 indicators include most of the standard stock market indexes, such as the Dow Jones average, the Standard & Poor's 500 average, and the advance/decline line. *Market Technician* plots the data in the stock files or the market indicator files, and can also superimpose a moving average line, a trend line, or a momentum line on the original. The program accepts data files from *VisiCalc* or other standard spreadsheet programs, provided the data is stored in the proper format. It can also transform its files into standard data interchange format (DIF) files for use on *VisiCalc*.

Figure 8-6. *Market Technician*

	Fair	Good	Very Good	Excellent
Ease of Use	☐	☐	☐	☑
Documentation	☐	☐	☐	☑
Reliability	☐	☐	☐	☑
Cost-effectiveness	☐	☐	☐	☑

Comments: The *Market Technician* should prove useful to many investors interested in technical analysis since it provides analysis of individual stocks as well as various market indicators—and because it also allows automatic updating of stock prices.

Market Technician's menu system is efficient and provides good screen prompts. Data entry, data file compiling, graphing, editing and searching, and creating stock files are supported from the main menu. A program disk, a market indicator database disk, and an instruction manual make up the *Market Technician* package. The manual is well-organized, fairly detailed, and includes a map of the eight program menus, with page number references. No index, however. This program is a "best buy" for members of the technical analysis school.

Note: Datamost, Inc. no longer sells *Market Technician*. However, you may still be able to find it in local computer stores or through various mail order companies.

Market Trend Analysis

Company: Personal Equity Management System
Computer: IBM PC (128K), IBM PC XT (128K)
Price: $350
Summary: *Market Trend Analysis* conducts tabulation and graphing of market indicators such as averages, prevailing interest rates, and investor psychological indicators (odd-lot short sales ratio, price of gold, and so on). It lets you track 87 technical stock market indicators—putting you in almost the same league as a professional technician.

These indicators are organized into three groups: technical, psychological, and fundamental. However, while most analysis programs let you automatically gather data from Dow Jones News/Retrieval or some other database service, you have to enter data manually with *Market Trend Analysis*.

Market Trend Analysis attempts to give you total market direction analysis. It reveals trends in the overall stock market by graphing data based on daily updates to almost 100 different time series to help you decide what direction the market will take in the upcoming months. If you're interested in investing, *Market Trend Analysis* can give you a look at trends, tell you what you could expect based on market psychology, and plot out moving averages, percentage changes, and divergence analyses.

The program uses information not available on most databases, so the company provides its own for updates. Unfortunately, this database costs $480 per year for monthly updates, or $60 per quarter to download the data from Personal Equity's computer.

N-Squared Market Analyzer

Company: N-Squared Computing
Computer: Apple II series (64K); IBM PC, IBM PC XT, IBM PC AT, (256K); IBM PCjr (128K); IBM PC-compatibles (256K)
Price: $295
Summary: *N-Squared Market Analyzer* is an interactive graphics program for analyzing market and financial data. It works with any uniform, periodic time series, such as stock or bond data.

The program comes with an updated data disk compiled from the Market Laboratory page of the weekly *Barron's* newspaper, going back to September 1980. You can quickly update this database either manually or automatically through a modem. In fact, you're not restricted to the data which comes with the program, for you can create your own database with any type of numerical data. The only restriction is that the data must be of the same frequency—you cannot mix daily, weekly, and monthly data in the same file.

You can choose 52, 70, 104, or 208 time periods. These numbers work best for weekly data, since most of them are multiples of 52, but you can opt for others. Arithmetic operations—addition, subtraction, multiplication, division, and exponentiation—can be selected and performed with any constant you choose. You can also perform the same operations with any two sets of data, as well as calculate percentages.

A number of other calculations are also available. They range from running sum and rate of change to log and user. The documentation adequately explains all of these operations, with examples. The User function even allows you to incorporate an expression of your own. Take a look at figure 8-7 for an example screen of *N-Squared Market Analyzer*.

Figure 8-7. *N-Squared Market Analyzer*

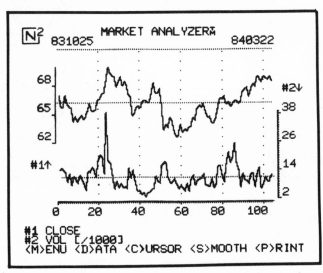

A 104-day chart produced by *N-Squared Market Analyzer*

Profit Stalker
Company: Button Down Software
Computer: Apple Macintosh (512K)
Price: $150
Summary: A technical analysis program using the graphics features of the Macintosh. *Profit Stalker* allows you to generate charts and graphs on a daily basis from your own database of price information. You can create bar charts, moving averages, and comparative trends, as well as resistance, momentum, oscillator, and other technical indicators.

Using the Macintosh, this program can display charts in a variety of formats. The chart windows can be moved, overlapped, or changed in size to better show comparisons.

Figure 8-8. *Profit Stalker* Screen

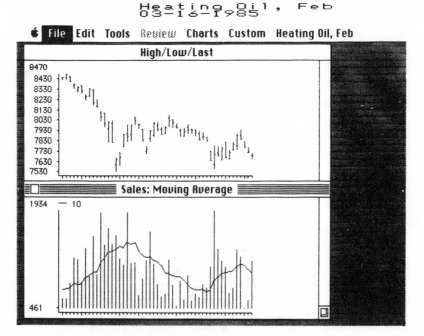

Charts can be locked, letting you print one over another. Here, a ten-day moving average is printed over daily volume.

Relative Performance

Company: International Algorithms
Computer: IBM PC
Price: $120
Summary: *Relative Performance* analyzes stock performance by looking at the percentage changes in price (up or down) over a maximum of 24 periods. These periods may be days, weeks, months, or other periods you select. Once the stock's name, symbol, closing price for the period, and change in price from the previous period are entered, the program calculates a *performance rating* for each period, ranging in value from -16 to $+16$. A *strength* value for the stock over the 24 periods is then calculated by summing the performance ratings for each of the periods. You can then use the strength value for each of the stocks in the portfolio to make buy or sell decisions.

Stock price data may be entered manually or automatically by using one of the several available databases. Up to 300 stocks may be entered into a database, each with as many price periods as desired. Only the latest 24 periods of data, however, are used in the relative performance analysis. *Relative Performance* displays or prints out the stock information, strength value, a new up-down price movement value, and a bar chart of up or down days ($+$ or $-$) for each stock.

Figure 8-9. *Relative Performance*

	Fair	Good	Very Good	Excellent
Ease of Use	☐	☐	☑	⟩ ☐
Documentation	☐	☐	☑	☐
Reliability	☐	☐	☑	☐
Cost-effectiveness	☐	☐	☑	☐

Comments: *Relative Performance* is a simple technical analysis program—but it doesn't conduct technical analysis in the usual way of plotting and analyzing stock prices over time. *Relative Performance* simply calculates a strength value for a stock, based on the percentage change in price of the stock over 24 periods. It's not possible to plot stock prices over time, and no further analysis of the price information is provided.

Relative Performance does not include a user's manual, data disk, or reference card. All that's provided is a single page of instructions and a fold-out flow chart of the main program steps.

Stock Strengths is a $15 evaluation package that contains a demo disk, a $20 discount coupon, descriptions, instructions, and a menu structure diagram. You can use *Stock Strengths* to decide whether to buy *Relative Performance*, the complete working program. *Stock Strengths* does all that *Relative Performance* does (create databases, display or print strongest or weakest past performers, and so on), but it won't update existing databases.

Right Time Stock Program
Company: TBSP, Inc.
Computers: Apple II series, IBM PC, IBM PC XT, IBM PC AT, IBM PC-compatibles
Price: $299
Summary: This technical analysis program bases its timing decisions/recommendations on a stock's price and volume. It generates a daily printout of the action to be taken for each stock. Each day, you enter the stock's volume and price manually or through Dow Jones News/Retrieval. The program calculates the 50-day moving average and provides a daily recommendation as a purchase, sale, or hold signal.

Stock Charting
Company: Diamond Head Software
Computer: IBM PC (128K)
Price: $70
Summary: *Stock Charting* creates charts to analyze a security's performance. It provides a moving average superimposed on actual price, and movements for the last 30 periods. Yield and price earnings can also be displayed. You can use a short period, 30 days, or a longer period, 30 weeks. *Stock Charting*

holds data for up to 30 stocks or other securities. Data is entered manually for each security. *Stock Charting* is evaluated in more detail in Chapter 10.

Stockie
Company: Logic Unlimited
Computers: Apple II series, IBM PC
Price: $125
Summary: *Stockie* bases its analysis on trading volumes and price fluctuations and is designed for the New York and American Stock Exchanges. Additionally, *Stockie* has the capabilities to plot mutual funds and over-the-counter stocks. The program provides a picture of the comparative amounts of resistance and support at each price level with a daily trend chart. This chart indicates the relative resistance (sell line) and support (buy line) of a stock. When the lines indicate large movements of resistance and support, the stock will have a dramatic price change.

As the price of a stock rises, more owners are willing to sell; this creates *resistance* to the price rise. Finally there are more sellers than buyers and the rise stops. This is also true of a falling stock. The lower the price, the more active buyers. This gives *support* to the falling prices.

The computer-adjusted charting is applied throughout the *Stockie* system, which includes daily trend analysis, price charting, and the combined trend chart.

Stock Market Advance/Decline
Company: Altman
Computer: Apple II series
Price: $149
Summary: This program uses daily and weekly advance/ decline values to make short (5–25 days) and intermediate term (3–13 weeks) market predictions. It's based on an extrapolative forecasting approach.

When using this approach, you're attempting to predict the future, based on the past. *Stock Market Advance/Decline* attempts to predict the future from published data—the number of stocks which advanced and the number of stocks which declined in price on the New York Stock Exchange. The theory is that these numbers indicate underlying market strengths or weaknesses.

Stock Market Advance/Decline calculates an advance/decline trend line and two exponential moving averages from either daily or weekly data. A change in the direction of the advance/decline line is signaled when the moving average lines cross. You must update the information to keep it current.

Neither indicator is disclosed—not the number of days included in the two moving averages, nor the extent of penetration of the advance/decline line necessary to generate a signal. The latter is not adjustable. Thus the program is only useful for investors dedicated to the advance/decline line as a primary market timing indicator.

Stock Mizer

Company: Mizerware (A & G Sales and Service)
Computer: IBM PC (128K)
Price: $130
Summary: *Stock Mizer* is a simple portfolio management and stock price analysis program. The program has three main sections: Stock Database Entry and Maintenance, Technical Analysis, and Portfolio Management.

The database lets you store a record of daily stock prices and trading volume for up to 30 stocks. The program can store 99 days of prices for each stock and allows you to to add, delete, and change the listing for any stock. The technical analysis module provides a set of five options—stock price line and bar graphs, stock trading volume line and bar graphs, 60-day moving average lines, 60-day price oscillator graph, and Granville price volume index—for the technical analysis of the price data stored in the database. Each of these graphs may be printed on the top or bottom of the screen, and one may be superimposed on another. The portfolio management section is a personal investment file system completely separate from the other modules. This section keeps a record of up to 200 individual stocks, including information on stock name, price, purchase or sale date, and commissions or fees.

Stock Mizer is menu-driven, with a main menu and submenus in each major segment. It can print a copy of each data file or graph, and it may be used with either color or black-and-white monitors.

Figure 8-10. *Stock Mizer*

	Fair	Good	Very Good	Excellent
Ease of Use	☐	☐	☑	☐
Documentation	☐	☑	☐	☐
Reliability	☐	☑	☐	☐
Cost-effectiveness	☐	☑	☐	☐

Comments: *Stock Mizer* is simple and easy to use, includes many of the more useful stock charting options, and lets you keep a record of personal investments. Stock price and volume information is easily entered (the program accepts prices in either decimal or fractional form) and the menu system is simple to follow.

Program initialization and startup, however, can be confusing. The proper procedure is not clearly described in the instructions. Rather than performing a simple system boot, you must first run BASIC A, then enter *Stock Mizer* with a LOAD statement.

Stock Trader
Company: DSF Software
Computer: IBM PC (with color monitor), IBM PC XT, IBM PC AT, IBM PC-compatibles
Price: $80
Summary: This basic technical investment analysis program may provide all the power you require. It can calculate, display, and print technical stock charts and moving averages. The trading signals generated by *Stock Trader* are based on three technical indicators, including a long-term moving average, a short-term moving average, and threshold for changes in the averages. You supply parameters which effect these three indicators.

The program can store up to 27 securities and 1 selected index (such as the Dow Jones). A simple four-page booklet serves as a starter manual, though you can also access the telephone support service. *Stock Trader* can provide a report for each stock or index. These reports contain information about the technical indicators you're generating under various parameters. It also makes good use of the printer by using boldface, italics, and regular print to highlight changes in a stock's prices.

You must collect data from the daily newspaper and enter it manually. The program is based on the system G. Appel and F. Hitscher outlined in their book, *Stock Market Trading System* (Dow Jones-Irwin, 1980).

Given its price, *Stock Trader* is worthy of consideration. To make it even more attractive, if you already own *Lotus 1-2-3* or *Context MBA*, DSF Software will include a portfolio manager template for $10 when you buy *Stock Trader*. (Most people will want to examine this program by first purchasing a demonstration disk for $6.95, which lets you use the full capabilities of *Stock Trader* for 15 trading days, and includes 30 days of data for eight stocks and the Dow Jones Industrial Average.

Technical Indicator Program

Company: Investment Software
Computers: Apple II series, IBM PC, IBM PC XT, IBM PC AT, IBM PCjr (128K)
Price: $69.50
Summary: The *Technical Indicator Program* is a standard technical investment analysis program which calculates, stores, and plots 18 technical stock market indicators based on a set of six entered items. The program also plots these six items. *Technical Indicator Program* does not store or plot any data for individual stock issues. The six required items include the number of advancing and number of declining issues, the advancing and declining columns, and the numbers of new highs and new lows. These items are most commonly taken from the New York Stock Exchange but they can be taken from any major exchange. All the data is entered manually.

The 18 technical stock market indicators calculated from this input data include the advance/decline line, McClellan oscillator, short and intermediate range, Magic T oscillator, Trader's Index, and several types of advance/decline and volume oscillators. You can plot any of these indicators on the screen or obtain a hardcopy printout. You can also prepare reports on some or all of the technical indicators calculated by the program.

Figure 8-11. *Technical Indicator Program*

	Fair	Good	Very Good	Excellent
Ease of Use	☐	☐	☑	☐
Documentation	☐	☑	☐	☐
Reliability	☐	☐	☑	☐
Cost-effectiveness	☐	☐	☑	☐

Comments: The *Technical Indicator Program* is reliable and easy to use, though not as sophisticated as some programs which provide for automatic updating from an investment database and plotting of individual stock prices. Still, it's useful in studying overall market indicators.

Menu-driven, the program is not well-documented, with few screen prompts or instructions. Program response is also fairly slow. The *Technical Indicator Program* package includes a program disk and an instruction manual. You have to supply the data disk. The instruction manual is highly detailed but not well-organized. The manual includes a brief discussion of each of the 18 technical indicators, as well as instructions on program operation. An index would be helpful, but one isn't provided.

The Apple version can be used under the ProDOS operating system, substantially speeding up the program. A file has been added to the Apple program to convert the week/day numbers to calendar dates and to print a list of week/day numbers and corresponding dates for each Monday of any year.

The IBM version includes an automatic run mode which allows an entire preselected set of charts to be printed. It also permits you to plot any number of weeks with a full-width chart and produces charts across year boundaries. Figure 8-12 shows an example of a *Technical Indicator Program* printout.

Figure 8-12. Printing Across Year Boundaries

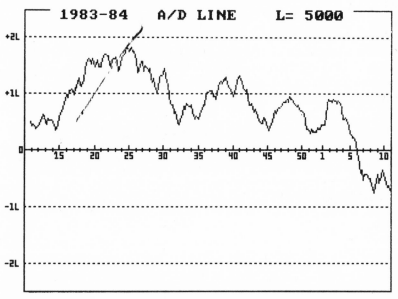

This plot shows how the IBM version of *Technical Indicator* can plot across the boundary of two years. The advance/decline line is used here as a technical indicator.

Technical Investor
Company: Savant Corporation
Computers: IBM PC XT, IBM PC AT (256K)
Price: $395

Summary: The *Technical Investor* is a standard technical investment analysis and data management program. It's divided into two main sections, the technical and the communications sections, with three further subdivisions within each.

The technical section includes data, chart, and file modules. The first—data—lets you create, edit, and manipulate a data file for a single stock or other security. Here the data is entered manually, although stock prices and other information may be automatically updated using a database accessed through communications. You can store up to 100 individual securities or 15,000 data entries on a single disk. Chart plots the price history of a security on one of four miniscreens and draws various technical indicator functions over this plot.

The *Technical Investor* contains many of the more important technical charting functions, including moving averages, exponential averages, regression lines, speed resistance lines, oscillator functions, trading bonds, and tracing volume indicators. You may plot more than one technical chart and stock price plot on each miniscreen, and each screen may be printed or saved to disk. The program also provides a number of charting control commands, which establish the parameters for the charting module. The files module simply allows you to display and print a list of all the security data files on a disk.

The communications section is divided into list, update, and terminal modules. List can create and edit a list of securities to be updated automatically from one of the database services. Update lets you automatically update stock price and volume data from either of two databases: Dow Jones News/ Retrieval or the Warner Computer Systems service. After defining the type of data to be retrieved and the files to be updated, you simply connect to the selected database and initiate an automatic file update. Terminal converts your computer into either a database terminal (for direct connection to Dow Jones or the Warner Computer service), or a general-purpose terminal (for connection to other databases by modem).

Figure 8-13. *Technical Investor*

	Fair	Good	Very Good	Excellent
Ease of Use	☐	☐	☐	☑
Documentation	☐	☐	☑	☐
Reliability	☐	☐	☑	☐
Cost-effectiveness	☐	☐	☑	☐

Comments: The *Technical Investor* is efficient and fairly easy to use. The program's main menu displays all available modules, which can be selected by moving a cursor and pressing the Enter key. The commands used in all but the chart module consist of either single function keys or groups of command keys. The command and charting function in the chart module, however, are overly complex and difficult to remember. Each consists of a two-letter code, which may or may not be related to the name of the underlying function, and often these commands must be joined together in strings separated by semicolons. In addition, no reference card or other aid listing the program commands is included with the system.

Technical Investor includes two master program disks (one for DOS 2.0, the other for DOS 1.1), one sample data disk, and an instruction manual. The manual is detailed, but not well-indexed—it includes few sample graphs or screen displays.

One unique feature of Technical Investor is its ability to split the screen into up to four miniscreens at any time during a charting and analysis session.

Figure 8-14. Miniscreens

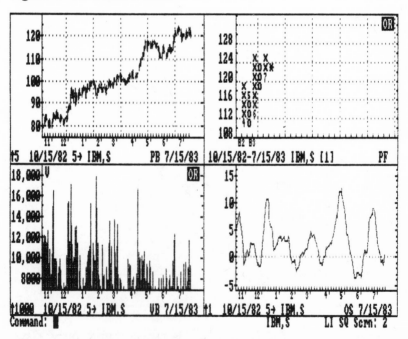

Just one example from Technical Investor, showing the program's ability to split the screen in up to four miniscreens as it charts and analyzes.

Overall, *Technical Investor* has the power even the most technically competent investor could want. *Technical Investor* is one of three programs in the Savant Investor Series. The other two are the *Fundamental Investor* and the *Investor's Portfolio*.

Winning on Wall Street—Trader's Forecaster

Company: Summa Software Corporation
Computers: Apple II series, IBM PC, IBM PC XT, IBM PC AT, IBM PC-compatibles
Price: $249 (Apple), $299 (IBM)
Summary: *Winning on Wall Street* is a set of modules useful for technical analysis, data communications management, and portfolio management. The *Trader's Forecaster* module is a technical analysis and forecasting tool. The *Trader's Data Manager* ($200) manages, stores information for the forecasting system, and can share information with the portfolio management system, *Trader's Accountant* ($350). Most users will want to consider purchasing the entire system for $700.

The *Trader's Forecaster* produces a wide variety of charts and graphs which permit you to carry out technical analysis. You can get a least-squares fit of the data, construct moving averages with trading bands, perform adaptive filtering, and construct speed resistance lines. Adaptive filtering can yield more accurate information than either straight moving averages or exponential smoothing, especially when the security you're evaluating has complex behavior patterns.

Forecaster charts the following volume indicators: negative volume, cumulative volume, price-volume trend, and daily volume. The last technical tool provided is another unique feature: point and figure charting capability. Point and figure charts are plotted based on a security's high, low, and closing volume. Technical traders use them to gauge a security's volatility.

Plots are made vertically, with Xs representing an up trend in the security and boxes indicating a down trend.

The charting speed is slow compared to other popular programs on the market. You spend too much time waiting for graphs or analyses to be plotted for a work session to be productive. However, the charts are crisp and provide excellent technical plots. Lastly, the total package price ($700) makes *Winning on Wall Street* considerably more expensive than its competitors. *Dow Jones Market Analyzer* ($350) includes a terminal feature, and *Market Analyst* (Anidata), which costs $495, has both terminal and portfolio management programs.

On balance, consider Dow Jones' *Market Analyzer,* Anidata's *Market Analyst,* the *Technical Investor,* or if you're really trying to keep costs down, the *Stock Trader.*

Figure 8-15. Support/Resistance Lines

This high/low/close/volume chart uses mid-channel support/resistance lines.

Investment Simulations and Games

Investment Simulations and Games

Modeling and simulation are of immense value to the investor because they permit one to study the effects of various decisions or choices *without* actually going through with the considered action. A *model* is a quantative representation of a process, showing the effects of those factors which are significant. Electronic spreadsheets, for instance, may be used to establish computer models.

Simulation is the use of a model to closely approximate the action of a system with many interacting parts. Flight simulators, for example, are regularly used to teach and sharpen piloting skills without actual flight. Stock market simulations allow an investor to try different courses of action without risking capital.

Market simulations should provide some insight into the operating principles of that market. The simulations and games listed in this chapter provide a low-cost experience with the market. They won't let you see the results of actual events on the actual price of real stock, but if the simulation is a good one, it *will* provide a certain feel about the financial markets and how you can operate within them.

How well these models emulate real life is open to question. At the very least, you can become familiar with financial terms—and be entertained while you do.

Beat the Street
Company: MEA Software Associates
Computer: Apple II series
Price: $50
Summary: *Beat the Street* is an investment game and technical analysis training program. Its purpose is to teach prospective investors technical analysis methods and investment decision-making by studying actual stock price charts.

The package includes a program disk, a data disk, and a set of instructions. Each data disk contains a five-year price history of 175 active common stocks. To play, you start the program and select one of the 175 listed stocks for charting. The program then slowly charts the daily price movements of the stock, using the point and figure method (X's for up movements, O's for down). You can stop the chart at any point to place a buy or sell order for the stock, or to reverse a previous order. *Beat the Street* displays both the running profit or loss on the players' trades and the final results when the simulation is finished.

You then select another stock to chart and the game repeats. The program does not store the results of any game, and only the stocks included on a data disk may be charted and traded. As an aid to interpreting the charts, the program displays hints such as *buy signal* and *sell signal*.

Figure 9-1. *Beat the Street*

	Fair	Good	Very Good	Excellent
Ease of Use	☐	☐	☐	☑
Documentation	☐	☐	☑	☐
Reliability	☐	☐	☑	☐
Cost-effectiveness	☐	☐	☐	☑

Comments: *Beat the Street* is a simple investment game, but it's effective in teaching the essence of technical investment analysis. The program is menu prompted and very easy to use. You may select a specific stock for charting or let the program choose one randomly.

Disks with several types of stocks are available, including disks with 175 New York Stock Exchange (NYSE) high tech stocks, 175 NYSE high volatility stocks, 175 American Stock Exchange stocks, or 175 over-the-counter stocks. The instructions supplied with the program explain the operation of the game but don't discuss technical analysis in detail.

The game is based on point and figure charting, a method of tracking the movement in stock prices. Case histories of 175 stocks are stored on the disk, and can be called up one at a time. On the screen you'll see a vertical string of X's, meaning the price is rising, or a string of O's, meaning the stock is falling. The object is either to buy or sell your stock at the optimum point, based on the movement you see on the screen.

The chart patterns develop as they actually appeared over time. The study of historic charts alone may develop a false sense of confidence in the method which often breaks down when faced with a critical market situation. *Beat the Street,* however, forces an interpretation of the price pattern as it unfolds. You'll quickly see if your interpretation is correct as later price activity is drawn on the screen.

In the real world, very few investors ever sell short—a serious shortcoming in developing trading skills. This simulation describes short selling in the text, and players are encouraged to practice selling short. The ability to recognize good short sale opportunities should give players a better feel for when to take profits on long positions. When to sell is probably the most important decision faced by long-term investors and practicing selling short should help develop the techniques you'll need to make effective decisions.

Comex
Company: Comex
Computer: IBM PC, IBM PC XT, IBM PC AT
Price: $70
Summary: *Comex* simulates gold and silver option trading by creating gold and silver option prices with historical futures price information, which includes a sophisticated options pricing model.

Beginners can learn how to create and test option trading strategies using combinations of calls, puts, and futures. Experienced traders can see how their gold and silver option strategies perform under real market conditions.

Computer Stocks and Bonds
Company: Avalon Hill Game Company
Computer: IBM PC
Price: $25
Summary: *Computer Stocks and Bonds* is an enjoyable and well-designed computer investment game. From one to six people can play, each beginning the game with $5,000. Each player tries to accumulate as much wealth as possible through the buying and selling of ten hypothetical stocks and bonds.

The player with the largest amount of money at the end of ten years or ten trading periods is the winner.

The program begins with a description of the game and the method of play. The number of players is selected, and the game begins. After a complete turn, the current investment portfolio of each player is displayed, as well as any dividends earned and each player's net worth. Players' final net worths are shown at the end of the game. At the start of each period, players may review the status of each stock or bond through a *securities review* option, and the program may also interject announcements of good or bad news about an investment. Bull or bear market conditions are randomly assigned at the beginning of each investment "year."

Figure 9-2. *Computer Stocks and Bonds*

	Fair	Good	Very Good	Excellent
Ease of Use	☐	☐	☐	☑
Documentation	☐	☐	☐	☑
Reliability	☐	☐	☐	☑
Cost-effectiveness	☐	☐	☐	☑

Comments: *Computer Stocks and Bonds* is an engaging investment game, neither too simple nor too complex. The random announcements of investment news and the assignment of a bull or bear market adds a realistic element of surprise to the game. The program is very easy to use, well-documented, and inexpensive. A complete set of screen instructions appears at the beginning of each game, which you may elect to view or skip. *Computer Stocks and Bonds* runs under BASIC A on the IBM PC and is easy to start up. Instructions are also included for running the game on other computer systems.

During each of the ten game years, players invest in securities at the current market price. To guide in selecting investments, players should frequently consult the securities review and price history graphs. Stock is sold only in blocks of ten shares. Player turn sequence is in net worth order—the wealthiest player goes first.

Millionaire

Company: Blue Chip Software
Computers: Apple II series, Apple Macintosh, Commodore 64, IBM PC, IBM PC XT, IBM PCjr, IBM PC-compatibles, TI Professional
Price: $39.95 (Commodore 64), $49.95 (Apple II series), $59.95 (all other versions)
Summary: *Millionaire*, a stock market simulator, is not based on random numbers, but on actual stock market trends and historical events. Each simulation is different from the last.

A game consists of 91 weeks, 13 of which have already passed by the time the game starts. Players are rated at five levels, determined by net worth. Higher levels permit more diverse investment opportunities. Fifteen stocks in five industries are available for trading.

On the Macintosh, player information is displayed in windows—up to four may be open at a time. Information players can consider includes the *Financial Journal*; stock market, industry, and company graphs; stock portfolio; and company profiles.

Figure 9-3. *Millionaire*

	Fair	Good	Very Good	Excellent
Ease of Use	☐	☐	☐	☑
Documentation	☐	☐	☐	☑
Reliability	☐	☐	☐	☑
Cost-effectiveness	☐	☐	☑	☐

Comments: *Millionaire* captures the uncertainty and risk in playing the stock market. The program is easy to use, and essentially self-explanatory. The manual includes a definition of terms and a glossary.

However, the game is not easy. If you're at a low player level, your investment options are limited to just stock purchases. As your net worth goes up, opportunities increase to call and put options and borrowing against net worth. Selling short is not permitted.

Figure 9-4. *Millionaire* on the Macintosh

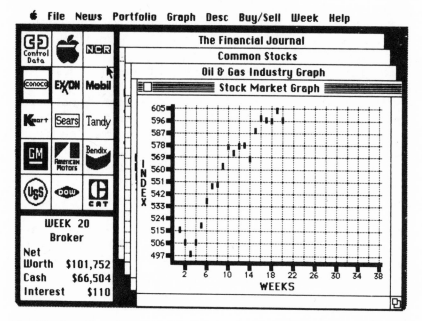

The Macintosh version of *Millionaire* uses impressive graphics and multiple windows.

Portfolio
Company: Flexible Software
Computer: Apple II series
Price: $48.95
Summary: *Portfolio* simulates the activities of a professional investment manager handling a portfolio of stocks, bonds, and commodities. The game is played by one player at a time; each game consists of a series of turns or moves around a game board.

You first negotiate your contract as an investment manager, then buy and sell stocks and bonds, buy commodities, take out loans for investment purposes, or buy personal luxury items.

No game board is shown on the screen; rather you make choices and review investment status by calling up a series of menus and tables on the screen. At the end of the game, the program compares the players' performances in managing a

154

$10 million portfolio to the performance of the computer opponent, and gives one of five awards if that performance was particularly good. A portfolio game may be saved on the program disk and completed later. A second player may even replay a saved game and compare his or her performance to that of the first. Up to 15 separate managers may store games on the program disk.

Figure 9-5. *Portfolio*

	Fair	Good	Very Good	Excellent
Ease of Use	☐	☐	☑	☐
Documentation	☐	☑	☐	☐
Reliability	☐	☐	☑	☐
Cost-effectiveness	☐	☑	☐	☐

Comments: As a mechanism for learning some of the important terms and strategies involved in investment management, *Portfolio* is fairly effective. As an entertaining and challenging investment game, however, *Portfolio* is not. The player moves slowly from screen to screen, making investment decisions, buying and selling stocks and bonds, and moving from turn to turn, but never has a feeling for the progress of the game. There's no clear opponent and no convenient running score to follow. You only learn of your relative performance at the end of the game.

Portfolio is menu-prompted and easy to use. The main menu allows you to start a new game, continue a stored game, view game descriptions, and inspect current managers. The package includes an instruction manual, a printed game board, a guide to the 15 artificial stocks, and a program disk.

The manual is somewhat confusing and doesn't clearly present the method of play or the process of making decisions. The instructions for running the program are included in back of the manual and are not clearly labeled.

One advantage of the game is that it lets you invest in stocks, commodities, *and* venture capital opportunities. *Portfolio*'s realism includes taxes. At year's end, your cash balance is compared to the previous year's, and the difference is taxed at 25 percent. At the end of each game, retiring investment managers receive letters from corporate headquarters summarizing their performances. The results are recorded in a player history file to be used as part of negotiations when the next game starts. In *Portfolio*, as on Wall Street, having a good reputation is worth money.

Tycoon
Company: Blue Chip Software
Computers: Apple II series, Apple Macintosh, Commodore 64, IBM PC, IBM PC XT, IBM PCjr, IBM PC-compatibles, TI Professional
Price: $39.95 (Commodore 64), $49.95 (Apple II series), $59.95 (all other versions)
Summary: A simulation of the commodities market, *Tycoon* displays a graph of the overall commodities index representing the 15 commodities in the game. You can speculate on gold, pork bellies, soy beans, wheat, cattle, and foreign currencies by means of contracts. You can even take short and long positions. Taking a long position means you believe the price is going to rise; if you think prices will fall, you'd take a short position. Although this is a simplified account of the commodities market, the game is still a learning experience.

In *Tycoon*, you can call up any of six graphs for each commodity: a bar chart of last year's monthly price changes; a scatter-plot graph of weekly price changes for the year to date; a three-week moving average of prices that smooths out price changes to help you spot trends; an oscillator graph to show net price change per contract; a point-and-figure graph to show upward and downward price movements; and a composite index of all commodities for the year to date.

You can also read the mock newspaper, the *Financial Journal*, which provides headlines such as "Farm agency says tight cattle supplies expected to continue."

The program requires that you devise flexible strategies, anticipate events, and then react as you trade in gold, silver, copper, oil, treasury bills, and foreign currencies, as well as agricultural commodities from wheat to soy beans. You're given comprehensive charts plus vital background data to aid you in spotting opportunities amid actual commodity price trends of the past.

Players start out as novices, with $10,000, trying to increase it to a million dollars. There are 15 commodities and currencies to choose from. You progress through six levels of difficulty which allow you to trade additional commodities. You can bypass these restrictions by electing the Cheater option when you begin.

You get weekly financial headlines and updated graphs for each commodity, including historical bar charts, a three-week moving average, and a point-and-figure chart. You then make transaction decisions. Your skill level and net worth are continuously displayed, and a portfolio report provides all the needed financial data, including cash and interest.

Tycoon is easy to use and realistic. You get onscreen explanations of each commodity contract, and the accompanying booklet even includes an introduction to futures trading, with tips on how to play.

Statistics
and Graphics

Statistics
and Graphics

Though charts are the basic tools of technical analysis, they're also useful for fundamental analysis and tracking securities. Charts and graphs can be powerful tools for reviewing the performance of a portfolio and for showing general market indexes. There are graphics capabilities available as part of several spreadsheet programs *and* there are excellent stand-alone programs. A separate graphics program gives you more flexibility and power, and often adds fine touches that characterize a professional piece of work. These advantages are often offset by the ease of use of graphics tied to a spreadsheet package.

Outstanding spreadsheet programs with integrated graphics include *Lotus 1-2-3* and *Super Calc 3*. They can be used to develop line, pie, and bar charts.

Superior stand-alone programs include *Apple II Business Graphics*, *The Graphics Department*, and *pfs: Graph*.

Advanced Chartist Plus
Company: Pardo Corporation
Computers: Apple II series, IBM PC, IBM PC XT
Price: $395
Summary: The *Advanced Chartist Plus* provides a complete set of graphic functions for the analysis of the stock and commodity markets. This software includes a graphics toolkit to create trend lines, price channels, and moving averages. You can extend lines and zoom in on any part of the graph. The program permits you to draw up to four moving averages. The advanced versions also allow you to create a wide range of indicators, such as fibonaci spheres, median line resistance, speed lines, on-balance volume, and relative strength.

Apple II Business Graphics
Company: Apple Computer, Inc.
Computer: Apple II series (64K, two disk drives, printer [optional])
Price: $175
Summary: *Apple II Business Graphics* is a well-developed and

easy to use business graphics program. It lets you present large volumes of business, financial, or other data in the form of complex graphs, bar charts, and pie charts. The data for a given figure is entered into a work file and the graph or chart is constructed using a number of simple commands. The Edit command enters data into a work file, Change changes the data in a file, Save stores the work file in a permanent disk file, and Draw Bar draws a bar graph of the data on the screen. Titles may be easily added to a figure with commands like Set Title or Set Horizontal Floating Title.

Apple II Business Graphics allows you to display figures on the screen or to print them out on four kinds of printers or plotters: the Houston Instruments DMP-3/4 digital plotter; the Hewlett-Packard 7225A/B digital plotter; the Qume Sprint 5/45 or 5/55 printers; and the Silentype printer. The program provides for either black-and-white or color figures, depending upon the type of display screen and plotter in use.

The *Apple II Business Graphics* program also allows the transfer of external data and text files (such as DOS 3.3 text files, Pascal/FORTRAN text files, and *VisiCalc* print files) into the program for display in a bar chart or graph.

Figure 10-1. *Apple II Business Graphics*

	Fair	Good	Very Good	Excellent
Ease of Use	☐	☐	☑	☐
Documentation	☐	☐	☐	☑
Reliability	☐	☐	☑	☐
Cost-effectiveness	☐	☐	☑	☐

Comments: *Apple II Business Graphics* is a flexible and sophisticated graphics program for the business user. With the aid of the tutorial section in the instruction manual, you'll be able to create useful and pleasing graphics within a few minutes. The process of entering numerous data points can be tedious but not difficult, and the program does provide for transferring data files from other software, such as the *VisiCalc* spreadsheet program. The ability to print complex charts and graphs, in color if you want, makes the program extremely useful for preparing figures for presentations and reports.

The program is very well-documented, with a complete instruction manual and a detailed reference card. The manual is divided into an easy-to-follow tutorial section in Chapter 2, followed by more detailed reference sections in Chapters 3 through 9.

Apple II Business Graphics also provides a complete set of help instructions. You can see additional instructions or advice simply by typing *Help* or *h*, followed by the name of the operation. To obtain additional information on drawing graphs, for instance, you'd simply type *Help Draw*.

The program contains a wealth of options for users to customize graphics for their own particular needs. Among these are the computation of averages; the ability to draw constant, linear, logarithmic, parabolic and sinusoidal curves (for charts based on predictions); and the ability to manipulate work-file data with dozens of different mathematical operations.

Apple II Business Graphics is a well-designed, powerful, and advanced tool. It's one of the better graphics packages currently available for the Apple. Keep in mind that since it's not menu-driven, less experienced users might find it intimidating. For users who can take advantage of its substantial power, however, it's an excellent tool.

Chart
Company: Microsoft Corporation
Computers: Apple Macintosh, IBM PC (with graphics card)
Price: $125 (Macintosh), $200 (IBM PC)
Summary: Compatible with *Multiplan,* this can be used in conjunction with that popular spreadsheet, or as a stand-alone program. An excellent tutorial is provided for the novice. On-screen help instructions are available.
Comments: *Chart* offers a lot of flexibility in arranging your own graphic presentation. For instance, you can move headings and legends around anywhere on the page, or change the patterns for each shaded area. The quality of graphics produced by *Chart* is largely determined by the printing device. Figures merely look good on a matrix printer—but they'll be outstanding on a plotter or a laser printer.

Figure 10-2. *Chart*

	Fair	Good	Very Good	Excellent
Ease of Use	☐	☐	☑	☐
Documentation	☐	☐	☑	☐
Reliability	☐	☐	☑	☐
Cost-effectiveness	☐	☐	☐	☑

Forty standard chart formats are available, all of which you can customize to suit your own needs. Ten types of charts, from pie to bar charts, are on call. Charts and graphs can be overlayed, expanded, and contracted.

Chart is compatible with other Microsoft products, such as *Word*, *File*, and *Multiplan*. Because of *Chart*'s compatibility with *Multiplan*, it's easy to move data from the spreadsheet in order to create graphics developed from your own calculations and information.

pfs: Graph
Company: Software Publishing Company
Computers: Apple II series, IBM PC
Price: $125
Summary: *pfs: Graph* can create line graphs, bar graphs, and pie charts. These can be produced from information provided by either *pfs: File*, *VisiCalc*, or from data entered directly from the keyboard. Up to four comparisons can be made on any one graph.
Comments: *pfs: Graph* is extremely easy to learn and use. It's also flexible and has a nice format. With the same set of data, any of the three types of graphs can be used. The fact that *pfs: Graph* can be used with *VisiCalc* makes it an even more attractive, powerful, and effective tool.

pfs: Graph comes with a disk, called Sampler, that's filled with a wide variety of prepared charts. The tutorial uses some of these charts in the examples. In addition to displaying each sample chart, you can see how its data is entered and how each is defined.

Figure 10-3. *pfs: Graph*

	Fair	Good	Very Good	Excellent
Ease of Use	☐	☐	☐	☑
Documentation	☐	☐	☐	☑
Reliability	☐	☐	☐	☑
Cost-effectiveness	☐	☐	☐	☑

The *pfs: Graph* manual introduces you to graphing basics that will smooth the way for understanding how the rest of the program works. There's a brief lesson explaining the X and Y axis (the horizontal and vertical lines of a graph) and how they're used, as well as an explanation of the three graph types available—bar, line, and pie—and their uses.

From the main menu of *pfs: Graph*, you can select one of six functions: Enter/Edit Data, Display Chart, Define Chart, Save Chart, Get/Remove Chart, and Print/Plot. One valuable feature is the ability to graph cumulative data. When this feature is selected, each point on the graph represents the total, or cumulative, Y value up to that point.

The Print/Plot routine allows any graph to be printed on a Silentype, Epson, or any other printer connected with a Grappler interface card. It may also be plotted on an HP 7470A Plotter.

pfs: Graph's value lies in its ease of use. If you need color graphs in the form of pie charts, bar graphs, or line graphs, this program may be just what you need.

Graphics Department
Company: Sensible Software, Inc.
Computer: Apple II series
Price: $125
Summary: The *Graphics Department* is a fairly sophisticated program for preparing line and bar charts and other kinds of business graphics. These charts may be presented on the computer screen—either as a single display or as a slide show consisting of a series of 32 different displays—or in printed form.

Printed graphics require the use of a Silentype printer and the appropriate printer interface program. Color graphics require a color monitor and color printer. The *Graphics Department* is a menu-prompted program with a main menu and several submenus. The main menu includes options for charting, lettering, graphics tools, the slide projector, printer interface, and file utilities.

The charting kit option lets you construct bar charts, line charts, pie charts, and scatter charts. It accepts data files from spreadsheet programs such as *VisiCalc*, provided the data is stored in data interchange format (DIF). If you want, you can enter the data manually. The program then displays the chart and stores the data in a file for future use. Each chart may contain up to 99 data points.

The next three main menu options allow you to modify and embellish the basic charts: You can add lettering to any chart, in up to 30 type styles or fonts; you can draw ellipses, points, and lines on any chart and "paint" portions of a chart displayed in hi-res graphics using the graphics tools; and with the slide projector, you can assemble a slide show of up to 32 different charts and tables. This may be timed so that the screen display changes at a preset interval.

Figure 10-4. *Graphics Department*

	Fair	Good	Very Good	Excellent
Ease of Use	☐	☐	☑	☐
Documentation	☐	☐	☑	☐
Reliability	☐	☐	☑	☐
Cost-effectiveness	☐	☐	☐	☑

Comments: The *Graphics Department* is a complex program with numerous options. It's fairly easy to enter data and draw simple line and bar charts; more effort is required to add detailed lettering to a chart or to prepare complex colored charts. The program is stored on three separate disks, which means some disk swapping has to be done to select the main menu options.

The package includes an instruction manual and three program disks. The manual is highly detailed but individual sections are not clearly marked. A glossary, instructions on running a brief demonstration program, a list of error messages, a list of available lettering styles, and an index complete the manual.

Instat
Company: Statistical Consulting Services
Computers: IBM PC (64K—*Instat*, 96K—*Instat-R*), IBM PC XT
Price: $45 (*Instat*), $95 (*Instat-R*), $25 (SCS.DAT)
Summary: *Instat*, *Instat-R*, and an associated file utility program, SCS.DAT, make up an elementary statistical analysis package. The *Instat* program provides for preliminary analysis of a statistical problem and preliminary screening of data. It can be used to screen investment information. *Instat* produces three types of displays: a frequency table, a histogram, and a mean plot. The mean plot function shows the mean for up to 100 groups of data, along with .50 and .95 confidence intervals and T-tests for all differences between means. *Instat* also preforms an elementary regression analysis if appropriate and plots a regression line on the mean plot.

Instat-R provides for the multiple regression analysis of one y-variable and as many as 29 x-variables. The program displays most of the statistics associated with multiple regression, including estimates and standard deviations of coefficients, p-values, residual sum of squared, and the standard deviation of the y-values about the regression line. Besides standard multiple regression, *Instat-R* supports forward stepwise, backward stepwise, backward elimination, and ridge regression. Plots of y-values, x-values, and residuals are all available and output may be sent to the screen, the printer, or to a file.

SCS.DAT is a file utility program for use with all of Statistical Consulting Services' programs. SCS.DAT lets you create or update a statistical data file, select specific values from a file, define fields in a file, modify old fields, change a field in file, and merge one file into another. SCS.DAT establishes data files in the format required of all the company's programs. SCS.DAT uses up to 50 variables per file.

Figure 10-5. *Instat*

	Fair	Good	Very Good	Excellent
Ease of Use	☐	☑	☐	☐
Documentation	☐	☑	☐	☐
Reliability	☐	☑	☐	☐
Cost-effectiveness	☐	☐	☑	☐

Comments: *Instat, Instat-R,* and SCS.DAT are fairly easy to use once you've mastered the command series. *Instat,* command-driven, works on one file at a time. A file is displayed, then manipulated using commands such as D (describe a variable), A (assign variable type), C (correlate), and T (tabulate). More complex functions require a series of commands and variable names. They're not that simple to master. *Instat-R* operates with a command screen which lists the functions, such as Regression; various options to be included in the analysis; and the variables to be analyzed. Options and variables are located and defined by moving an active cell with the arrow keys. SCS.DAT, however, is quite easy to use.

Each program includes a detailed instruction manual with an index and a brief command guide. The manuals describe each function or command in some detail, but only a few examples are given and no sample screen displays are included. No reference cards or sample printouts are provided.

The major advantage of *Instat* and *Instat-R* is that they provide a way to analyze elementary data. Data may be displayed and analyzed in a preliminary way, in preparation for further analysis in these programs, or in more sophisticated programs run on larger computers. The disadvantages of these programs are that they can support only preliminary statistical analysis of relatively small data sets and that they require considerable knowledge of statistics to be efficiently used. The instruction manuals attempt a cursory explanation of each statistical procedure and test, but are far from satisfactory and are difficult to follow if you're not intimately familiar with statistics.

Market Illustrator
Company: N-Squared Computing
Computer: Apple II series
Price: $195
Summary: This program complements *N-Squared Market Analyzer* (see Chapter 8). *Market Illustrator* provides two programs for plotting and comparing individual stocks and commodities with major market indicators and with some 164 data files grouped under 20 major categories of market information. Files can be created, deleted, edited, modified, merged, and updated. Data from any two files can be selected, exponentially smoothed, and plotted for any of three different time periods.

You can develop comparison graphs between alternate investments, compare performance data on dissimilar types of investments, or check performance against the forces that influence the market (such as the prime rate). For example, you can chart the effect of the prime on the Dow Jones Industrial index. Making the charting even more specific is also possible—if you want, you can compare the prime rate to the performance of farm equipment stocks.

Market Illustrator also includes a graphics generating program which constructs single issue charts for stocks and futures. The performance of commodities futures or individual stocks for up to 160 trading days can be plotted on a graph.

An auto-run mode lets you preselect data files to be compared to one another; the mode also generates a new graph about every 30 seconds. Graphs may be sent to the screen, printer, or disk.

Individual stock data files can be created and updated using historical data downloaded from CompuServe, Dow Jones, or another service. Closing prices are plotted on the upper portion of the screen, and volume is plotted on the lower portion. You may select line, dot, or bar plotting, and multiple plots may be overlayed on one chart. Additional plotting features include automatic scaling of graphs, viewing two graphs on a split screen, or one graph on a single screen.

The documentation, programming, error detection, and error handling are well-executed. The manual is well-written, organized, and edited. Explanations and descriptions are clear and concise.

StatPro

Company: Wadsworth Software
Computers: IBM PC, IBM PC XT
Price: $795
Summary: *StatPro* is a menu-driven statistics program which makes it easy to enter data and format into the database. The automatic error-checking features include range checking and verification. You set a range by giving the minimum and maximum values for each.

StatPro has a convenient data manipulation feature that includes preprogrammed unit conversions, such as degrees Fahrenheit to degrees Centigrade. You can also define your own transformations. Data can be manipulated by using general algebraic formulas, normal variates, and coordinate transforms.

StatPro's statistical routines are arranged into five groups: descriptive statistics, regression, analysis or variance (ANOVA), time-series, and multivariate analysis. Using the routines is easy, primarily because of the excellent menus. After you select an analysis, you simply give the criteria for record selection and processing options. Options include details about what should be computed, such as particular descriptive statistics or nonlinear regression. Of particular interest to investors are the time-series analysis routines, including a moving average routine and an exponential forecasting routine. These analyze chronological data, such as stock market listings or reports of seasonal purchasing behavior.

Stock Charting

Company: Diamond Head Software
Computers: IBM PC, IBM PC XT, IBM PC AT (all need color graphics capabilities), IBM PCjr (128K)
Price: $70
Summary: *Stock Charting* is a simple program for plotting the price of a stock over a 30-day period, and for calculating and plotting a moving average estimate of stock price over the same period. The program plots the high, low, and closing price for each day; plots the moving average trend line; and at the bottom of the screen, plots the total volume of the stock

traded in each of the 30 days. The program can hold the price data for 20 stocks per disk, but can hold only 30 days' (or periods') prices per stock. If a new day's price is added, the earliest day's price is lost. *Stock Charting* also prints the current yield, current price/earnings ratio, and estimated price earnings ratios for the next two years. You must manually enter this financial data and the 30 days of stock prices (see below for exception).

Figure 10-6. *Stock Charting*

	Fair	Good	Very Good	Excellent
Ease of Use.	☐	☐	☑	☐
Documentation	☐	☑	☐	☐
Reliability	☐	☑	☐	☐
Cost-effectiveness	☐	☐	☑	☐

Comments: *Stock Charting* is a straightforward graphics program. When used with the required IBM PC system (color display, color graphics board), it provides dramatic plots of a stock's price and sales volume over a 30-day period.

Documentation consists of an instruction book, which describes the procedures for adding and deleting a stock, updating stock prices, scaling a stock's prices for a stock split, and printing data and plots for a stock. It also briefly describes the meaning of the moving average trend line. The program is fairly limited in scope, however, since it can only record and plot price data for 30 days at a time, and only perform one type of analysis: the moving average. One additional inconvenience is that you must copy the DOS command, BASIC A, and graphics program files from the DOS system disk onto the *Stock Charting* disk before running the program. The DOS graphics program file must be copied onto the *Stock Charting* disk to print displayed stock charts.

Figure 10-7. Printing with *Stock Charting*

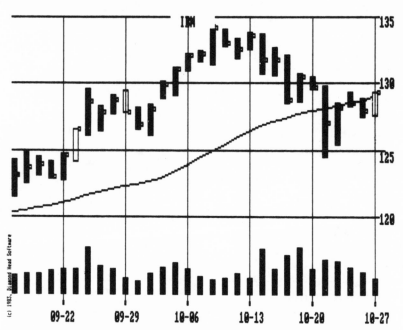

Chart of a 30-day period showing IBM's high, low, and closing price for each day (top), a moving average trend line (middle), and the total volume of stock traded (bottom).

Diamond Head Software has entered into an agreement with Warner Computer Systems which permits *Stock Charting* to access Warner's database and download data. No additional communications software is necessary. Nonprime time access to the database (at 300 bps) costs $.30 per minute. Data is downloaded, stored on disk, and entered into your portfolio. If you prefer, it can be manually updated thereafter.

Stox

Company: Stockware Systems
Computer: Apple II series
Price: $70
Summary: *Stox* is a simple data management and stock price charting program. *Stox* stores the closing price and trading volume for up to 12 stocks on each disk, prints or displays a chart, and prints a report of the information on each stock. The program stores up to 140 weeks of data on each stock. The program also calculates and plots a moving average line for each currently displayed stock price chart.

All the data stored and printed by *Stox* must be manually entered—no automatic updating of data is possible. The program allows you to add, update, and erase stocks from a current file; change filenames; and adjust stock prices for a stock split.

Figure 10-8. *Stox*

	Fair	Good	Very Good	Excellent
Ease of Use	☐	☐	☑	☐
Documentation	☐	☑	☐	☐
Reliability	☐	☐	☑	☐
Cost-effectiveness	☐	☑	☐	☐

Comments: *Stox* is an efficient but simple stock price charting program. Its simplicity means you're limited in the number of functions and storage space. There are many investment analysis programs currently available that provide a large number of complex functions, and much more storage space, for prices not much greater than *Stox*'s. Many of these other programs also provide for automatic updating of stock prices from electronic databases, something *Stox* cannot do.

The menus of *Stox* offer options ranging from loading data from disk and reviewing data to drawing new graphs and adding moving averages. The program package includes a program disk, a data disk, and an instruction manual. The latter provides a complete description of the program, a brief tutorial, and an index.

Figure 10-9. *Stox* at Work

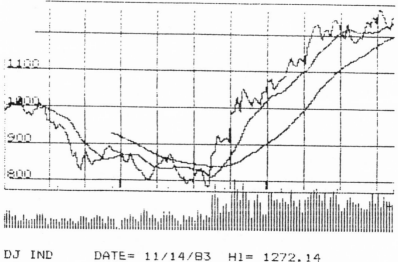

```
DJ IND        DATE= 11/14/83    HI= 1272.14
13 WK MA      LAST= 1233.24     LO= 784.34
AVOL= 3221    LVOL= 1473        CL= 1250.18
```

Stox's charts include the date, high, low, close, last bid, low volume, and average volume. Note the moving average lines.

Bonds and Mutual Funds

Bonds and Mutual Funds

Bonds

A *bond* is a certificate of debt issued by a government or corporation, guaranteeing payment of the original investment, plus interest, by a specified date. Calculations necessary to evaluate bonds and portfolios of bonds are somewhat complex, but computer programs have helped buyers and sellers for years.

Although bond market analysis has been the domain of professional money managers who invest institutional portfolios, some of the new application packages, such as *Bond Scholar*, are designed for the typical account executive or individual investor who wants to manage a bond portfolio, do calculations, and keep on top of the fixed-income market.

Instead of thinking of bonds as long-term investments, as many investors do now, personal computers and their software may make it possible for you to practice short-term investing, moving in and out of bond investments, just as you can with stocks.

Bond Scholar

Company: Investech, Inc.
Computers: IBM PC, IBM PC XT, IBM PC AT, IBM PCjr, IBM PC-compatibles (all require 128K)
Price: $1,995 for *Basic Bond Scholar;* $500 each for *Swap Analysis, Reinvestment Rate Scan, Portfolio Evaluator,* and *Mortgage* modules
Summary: *Bond Scholar* consists of five modules—*Basic Bond Scholar, Swap Analysis, Reinvestment Rate Scan, Portfolio Evaluator,* and *Mortgage.*

Basic Bond Scholar computes prices, cash flow yields, yields to maturity, and after-tax yields. *Swap Analysis* evaluates possible swaps between two fixed income securities. *Reinvestment Rate Scan* scans and plots graphs, showing total return on up to three different securities at once. The *Portfolio Evaluator* module summarizes average coupon, duration, and other statistics on a portfolio of bonds.

Basic Bond Scholar provides comparisons of all fixed income investment alternatives after taxes and reinvestment of cash flows under any tax/reinvestment scenario you choose. The common denominator is the Par Bond Equivalent (sometimes called the Current Coupon Equivalent). It's a single yardstick that compares all types of cash flows from varied and complex reinvestment options which are hard to compare otherwise.

BondWare
Company: Davidge Data Systems Corporation
Computers: IBM PC, IBM PC XT, IBM PC AT, IBM PC-compatibles (requires 128K and at least one 320K disk drive; DOS 2.0 and above for all versions)
Price: $450
Summary: *BondWare* provides a yield calculator, portfolio analyzer, and swap analysis for fixed income securities. Municipal bonds, corporate bonds, treasury bills, mortgages, GNMA bonds, and certificates of deposits (CDs) can be analyzed.

The yield calculator includes current yield, call yields, and realized compound yield. Any bond entered into the yield calculator screen can be saved in a portfolio file to create a portfolio analysis report. Special features of the portfolio analyzer allow weighted averages computed on the bases of par value, market value, or cost; customer names, addresses, and effective tax rates stored in files for easy printing on analysis reports; and portfolio summaries which show market value and capital gain situations. Ratings can be stored, and weighted averages computed from a user-customized rating file; portfolio reports can be printed to disk files to include in documents; and a utility program reformats saved bond portfolios for placement into *Lotus 1-2-3* spreadsheets.

The *BondWare* portfolio swap evaluator tabulates complete results of single or multiple bond swaps, including all changes shown on absolute and percentage bases and all changes shown on both pre- and after-tax bases.

Financial Software Series
Company: Technical Data Corporation
Computers: IBM PC, IBM PC XT, IBM PC AT, IBM PCjr, IBM PC-compatibles (all require 192K)
Price: $6,980 (all five programs at 20 percent discount)

Summary: The *Financial Software Series* is a set of five highly sophisticated programs for analyzing fixed income securities. The program is primarily intended for the professional bond fund manager, securities analyst, and financial officer.

The five programs include *Yield Calculator, Bond Swap Analyzer, Rate of Return Analyzer, Fixed Income Portfolio Manager,* and *Mortgage Calculator.* These may be purchased individually or as a complete package—you'll receive a 20 percent discount on the total price if you buy four or more. The *Financial Software Series* lets you analyze all the most important types of fixed income securities, such as government, corporate, agency, and municipal bonds; money market instruments; Euro bonds; certificates of deposit; and most types of mortgage-backed pass-through securities. Before any analysis is conducted, you first must enter information on each of the bonds, and place it into the Issue File. You can type in this data or automatically retrieve it from the Chase Econometrics/Interactive Data Corporation database. Up to 400 issues may be stored on a single disk.

Yield Calculator is essentially a powerful bond calculator. It calculates the yield to maturity, after-tax yield to maturity, current yield, price, duration, and several other variables for each issue in the file. A range option calculates and displays a table of up to 40 yields and prices for each bond, based on the starting value and increment you choose. *Bond Swap Analyzer* evaluates the consequences of a proposed bond swap. It evaluates a swap of up to ten fixed income securities on both sides of the transaction (buy and sell) and calculates the yield or price, duration, accrued interest, after-tax yield, and yield at cost for each. It calculates and graphs a yield curve for the rates of return of up to 14 selected bond issues. These may be Treasury issues or any of the other fixed income securities accepted by the series. You can graph and compare up to four separate yield curves at once, each calculated on a different set of horizon date and reinvestment rate assumptions. *Rate of Return* also lets you calculate the rate of return achieved by any issue portfolio.

Fixed Income Portfolio Manager is simply a portfolio data management program. It allows you to form up to 32 separate portfolios from the Issue File, as well as prepare reports and display the information in each. Finally, *Mortgage Calculator*

179

figures the yield-to-cash flow, rates of return, and other variables for all of the mortgage-backed pass-through securities in the file.

Figure 11-1. *Financial Software Series*

	Fair	Good	Very Good	Excellent
Ease of Use	☐	☐	☑	☐
Documentation	☐	☐	☐	☑
Reliability	☐	☐	☐	☑
Cost-effectiveness	☐	☑	☐	☐

Comments: The *Financial Software Series* is a powerful and sophisticated set of investment programs which provides you with many options and methods of analysis. But since they deal with a rather complex area of investment analysis, they're not easy to use or to understand at first. You'll need to spend some time with them before you'll be able to utilize their full potential.

The series is generally well-designed and gives you considerable help in analyzing information. The data file system (Issue File), is particularly easy to use. All of the issues are stored in a single data file. The issues may then be formed into a parallel set of portfolios and analyzed as a group, or each issue may be analyzed separately by each of the five programs.

The system is organized as a series of main menus and submenus. Movement between menus is simple and the programs offer a good set of screen prompts. Nearly all of the commands consist of single numbers, letters, or command keys. A help command, providing more instructions for using a program, is also available on some menus.

When you buy the *Financial Software Series*, you receive a main program disk, a *Mortgage Calculator* program disk, a data disk, and an instruction manual. The manual provides a fairly complete description of the operation of each major program, including many sample screen displays and reports. Very little discussion is provided on the meaning or interpretation of the financial variables calculated by the programs, however. The package also includes a quick reference guide.

Master Brain Bond Calculator
Company: Decision Programming Corporation
Computers: Apple II series, IBM PC, IBM PC XT, IBM PC AT
Price: $375
Summary: This program aids the investor in the selection and trading of bonds by computing yields, reinvestment rates, capital gains, and future price projections. It also does IRA, future value, and annuity calculations and predicts the impact of various rate adjustments. One feature of note is its ability to help you decide whether to sell a bond before it matures. The impact of income and capital gains taxes can also be easily factored into any analysis. The program's drawback is that data cannot be stored on disk, though it can be printed on paper.

Figure 11-2. Good News?

"I'm pleased to tell you your portfolio is outperforming the market. For that matter, so is your grocery store."

Mutual Funds

A *mutual fund* is a company which uses the funds of many people with similar investment goals and invests these funds, for these people, in a wide variety of securities. Each shareholder, in effect, owns a part of a diversified portfolio of securities and has a professional manage that portfolio.

There are mutual funds which invest in fixed income securities, money market investments, and stocks. The investor in a mutual fund or set of mutual funds is interested in tracking the performance of his or her portfolio by accounting for dividends, capital gains, and the net asset value of the funds.

Fund Master TC

Company: Time Trend Software
Computer: Apple II series, IBM PC, IBM PC XT, IBM PC-compatibles
Price: $190 (Apple), $210 (IBM)
Summary: *Fund Master TC* lets you analyze mutual funds on your own personal computer. The program has the capacity to record and store daily prices of up to 100 mutual funds. To obtain price information on a mutual fund, you can use the package's telephone update service to link to Dow Jones News/Retrieval. Once the price information has been recorded, you can perform any one of a number of analyses on each mutual fund.

Such analyses include a display of a fund's price over time and a display of exponentially smoothed moving averages for each fund (in chart form) using several market indicators. Each of these provides valuable information in determining the performance of a mutual fund.

Comments: *Fund Master TC* is a fairly simple program for storing and analyzing data on mutual fund investments. The program stores the closing prices of a portfolio of mutual funds, charts the closing prices of a fund over time, and ranks the portfolio according to a momentum index. The mutual fund closing price data may be entered manually or updated automatically through Dow Jones News/Retrieval. *Fund Master TC* also stores and charts data on five common stock market indicators, including the advance/decline line and an index of your choice.

Figure 11-3. *Fund Master TC*

	Fair	Good	Very Good	Excellent
Ease of Use	☐	☑	☐	☐
Documentation	☑	☐	☐	☐
Reliability	☑	☐	☐	☐
Cost-effectiveness	☑	☐	☐	☐

Fund Master TC is a unique software package—it's extended the concept of portfolio management to mutual funds. The package isn't really acceptable, however, since it has too many defects. Numerous (even excessive) errors occur when you run the program, including syntax errors. You run into these errors again and again when you use *Fund Master TC*.

Fund Master TC's documentation doesn't help, either. The explanations of the program's functions are so brief that you're often unable to figure out their purpose. When a program is this difficult to operate, documentation should attempt to clarify its features.

Unfortunately, a revised version of *Fund Master TC* shows a number of fatal program errors similar to those in the earlier version. Two copies of the master program disk were run and each displayed the same errors. In particular, the program crashed and displayed an error message when it was asked to print the entire price history for a specific mutual fund, when the space key was pressed rather than the Return key when asked to print another file, and when the Return key was pressed when the Market Indicator menu was on the screen. The program was generally difficult to run; and when it ran, it ran slowly.

Futures and Options Contracts

Futures
and
Options Contracts

The Futures Market

The volume of futures contract trading in the United States has mushroomed since the late 1950s. In 1983 alone, almost 100 million futures contracts were traded. The reason for this growth is twofold: More and more people are turning to futures trading as a way to beat inflation, and the number of contracts available for trading continues to grow with each year. In addition to the traditional so-called primary commodities, such as grains and metal, markets also exist for live animals, processed commodities, foreign currencies, mortgage interest rates, U.S. Treasury bonds, and stock index futures. And there are even more planned. All these commodities and financial instruments are traded in what is known as the *futures market.*

Whenever something is ordered instead of bought on the spot, a *future contract* is involved. The price is decided at the time the order is placed, but cash is only exchanged later. For example, when a bushel of wheat is sold, the exchange takes place in the cash market. In that case, the bushel changes hands as cash is paid to the seller. The transaction takes place and for all practical purposes is completed then and there. Most traditional securities are traded in this type of market.

But a bushel of wheat could also be sold in the futures market. Then the seller would not actually deliver the wheat until a mutually agreed-upon date. The transaction would not be completed for some time; the seller would receive partial payment for the wheat at the time of the agreement, and the balance on delivery. The buyer, in turn, would own a highly liquid futures contract that could be held (and presented for delivery of the bushel of wheat), or even traded in the futures market. No matter what the buyer does with the contract, as long as it's outstanding, the seller has a legal and binding obligation to deliver the stated quantity of wheat on a specified date at an agreed price.

The essence of a futures contract is standardization. For example, the Chicago Board of Trade specifies the requirements for its commodities' contracts. A commodity exchange sets all the terms of a futures contract but the price, and then authorizes trading in it.

In actual practice, the various commodity markets allow the producer or consumer to establish a fixed price that will be paid or received for a given commodity at a future date. The contract standardizes the quantity and quality of the commodity traded, and specifies the future month of delivery and the price to be paid. Unlike an option contract, which gives you the *right* to buy or sell at a given price, a futures contract *commits* you to buy or sell at that price. That price is called the *exercise* price, or since it is "struck" when the buyer and seller negotiate terms, it's sometimes called the *striking* price.

Commodity markets were initially developed to satisfy food producers' needs, and are usually associated with foodstuffs and with precious metals. Some major exchanges are the Chicago Board of Trade (CBT) for grains, the New York Commodities Exchange (Comex) for metals, and the Chicago Mercantile Exchange for cattle and hogs.

In the past few years, an increasing number of financial futures markets have developed. The International Money Market (IMM) offers foreign currency futures, the Chicago Board of Trade now offers government securities, and the Kansas City Board of Trade provides a futures market for the price of the Value Line Stock Index. These futures contracts are simply commitments to buy or sell a financial instrument for a certain price during a specific time period. The most widely traded future is one on the Treasury bond.

Future contracts based on indices of stock markets such as the Standard & Poor's 500 or the New York Stock Exchange are also available. Stock index futures contracts are especially well-suited to both technical analysis and day-trading. Since stock indexes are composites, they move up and down smoothly and move consistently with smaller increments per move. Stock index futures first began trading in 1982. There are now three separate stock indexes on three different commodity exchanges. The Standard & Poor's Index is traded on the Chicago Mercantile Exchange; the New York Stock Exchange Composite Index is traded on the New York Futures

Exchange; and the Value Line Index is traded on the Kansas City Board of Trade.

Futures contracts are primarily financial instruments that create an obligation to buy or sell an underlying item, in this case nothing more concrete than an abstract index. Since there is nothing to take or deliver, all obligations are settled in cash. Participants are simply hedging positions and/or speculating on trends on the overall performance of the markets.

Option Contracts

An *option* is a contract conveying the *right* to buy or sell designated securities or commodities at a specified price during a stipulated period. It is an agreement between two parties in which one grants the other the right, but not the obligation, to buy or sell under stated conditions. The party retaining the option (the one which has to make a choice of whether to buy or sell) is usually called the *option buyer.* The party with no choice is the *option seller,* sometimes called the *writer* or *maker* of the option.

The most prominent type of option is named the *call* option. It gives the buyer the right to "call away" a specified number of shares of a given security. A *put* is an option to sell a stock to the option seller at a specified price, up to a given expiration date.

In recent years there have been markets established for the trading of options on stock index futures. These are yet another step removed from the securities themselves. In this case, the options give the purchaser the right, but not the obligation (as with commodities), to buy or sell the stock index futures. These options are no different from those on sugar, wheat, gold bullion, or financial obligations: Puts give the owner the right to sell the index to the writer of the options contract, and calls give him or her the right to buy the indexes within the duration of the contract. The prices of these options are also determined in the open market, based on such things as the value of the index shares, the length of the option's life, and immediate economic prospects. These index options are a hedge on the overall direction of the market as measured by the Standard & Poor's 500, the Value Line, or the New York Stock Exchange Composite indexes.

The value of an option is based on the present value of the exercise price and the stock dividend prior to the options expiration date. Professors Fisher Block and Myron Scholes developed the widely used Black-Scholes valuation formula in 1973.

Whether trading instruments such as options and futures serve an economic purpose depends on who you talk to. While they can provide for hedging, most participants are clearly speculators. This may change as these markets mature and are better understood. However, within the first year or two of activity their popularity surprised everybody—50,000 index contracts with a face value of more than $3 billion are being traded daily. On some days the volume on index futures has exceeded that of the New York Stock Exchange. Clearly, there are many investors interested in trading futures contracts for stock indexes as well as commodities.

With the proper software and your personal computer, you can trade with a bit more confidence. These programs, like their counterparts in fundamental and technical analysis, take a variety of indicators into consideration. And like the other programs in this book, they vary in their expertise and sophistication.

Auto Trader

Company: Avinco Corporation
Computer: IBM PC, IBM PC XT, IBM PC AT, IBM PCjr, IBM PC-compatibles (192K recommended for all computers)
Price: $50
Summary: *Auto Trader* assists in the trading of commodity futures contracts. When given a price history of a contract and your defined strategy, it provides daily recommendations on each contract. It tells you the price to buy and the price to sell. The approach is based on the theory that opportunities can be uncovered by comparing the day's trading range for a commodity with a closing-price moving average. You can choose 5, 8, or 30 day averages.

When a market changes direction, the actual price of the commodity will, at some point, cross the moving average. In a market that's been falling, this would be a good time to buy. Alternatively, the market may continue to fall, and the price rise which crossed the moving average may have indicated just a temporary rally. In that case, it would have been a good time to sell.

Auto Trader's recommendations are based on strategy that you define, and on the application of that strategy to a price history. By comparing the daily price range to the moving average, *Auto Trader* generates buy or sell recommendations. The most important element in the trading strategy is your choice of how many days to include in the moving average. You specify the number of days and a factor related to how aggressively you want to trade. The actual method used by *Auto Trader* in providing the recommendation, however, isn't really apparent.

Fair Value Commodity Options System
Company: Software Options, Inc.
Computers: IBM PC, IBM PC XT, IBM PC AT, IBM PC-compatibles
Price: From $2,950
Summary: A modular commodity options analysis program. It includes a valuation module that calculates theoretical values, time and intrinsic values, hedge ratios, and fair values. This also produces color graphs to illustrate the options data. The advanced option trading module produces matrices of data for different option maturities and striking prices, while the option strategies module displays a worksheet for entering strategies on up to five trades. The portfolio manager maintains records and results.

The various modules analyze almost any option, from those on futures and stock indices to those on stocks and currencies.

FutureSource
Company: Commodity Communications Corporation
Summary: An information and database for commodities contracts. (See Chapter 4 for a complete description.)

Options Analyst Plus
Company: Datalab, Inc.
Computer: Apple II series, IBM PC, IBM PC XT, IBM PC AT, IBM PC-compatibles
Price: $450 (stock version), $350 (nonstock version)
Summary: *Options Analyst Plus* provides option screening and strategy analysis. The stock version of the program covers options on 358 listed optionable stocks, while the nonstock

version covers options on stock indices, stock index futures, interest rates, foreign currencies, Treasury bonds, and commodities. The program provides valuation calculations and strategy analyses, and is supported by a complete data service or disk mailed to subscribers on a twice-monthly basis. Current market prices can be entered manually or accessed through a modem.

Options-80A
Company: Options-80
Computers: Apple II series, IBM PC, MS-DOS computers, Tandy 2000, TRS-80
Price: $170
Summary: *Options-80A* analyzes buying and selling of listed call and put options and spreads. The effects of commissions, cost of money, dividends, and risk exposure are included. The program also provides the annualized percent return on investment.

Aimed at the individual investor, the *Options-80A* version features Black-Scholes modeling to determine theoretical option prices and return on investment. Enhancements also include put/spread analysis, expanded covered writing of call options, and flexibility in design and printing of plots and graphs. *Options-80A* is a sound program for the option trader who is trying to maximize returns.

Optionsware
Company: J.C. Productions
Computers: Apple II series, Commodore 64, IBM PC, IBM PC XT, IBM PC AT, IBM PCjr
Price: $350
Summary: This program can be used for short-term trading of the Standard & Poor's 100 Index options contracts (OEX). *Optionsware* uses six items of data: Standard & Poor's 100 high, low, and close; NYSE advance/decline; and NYSE volume. The program makes predictions and gives buy/sell recommendations on puts and calls. It also recommends what days to buy for the predicted profit, and maximum price to pay.

This short-term trading predictor results in trading in one to seven day periods. It claims a 75 percent success rate in predicting 300 transactions over a 16-month period.

OptionX
Company: Crawford Data Systems
Computers: Apple II series, Apple III
Price: $145
Summary: *OptionX* is a sophisticated program for calculating the correct price of a stock option. It supports two different pricing models, the Black-Scholes option pricing formula and the Cleeton option pricing formula.

OptionX runs from a single main menu, which has selections such as Option Analysis, Volatility Analysis, Expiration Calendar Review, Initial Conditions Review/Change, Stock Data Review/Change, Brokers Commission Schedule, and Days Between Dates. The various program functions include the type of option model, the current risk-free rate of interest, the date, the broker, and the option commission discount. These conditions may be changed at any time.

The Stock Data selection lets you store basic option pricing information for a set of frequently analyzed stocks on the program disk. Option Analysis, however, is the heart of the program. It allows you to calculate the correct option price for a number of options on a specific stock using either of the modeling methods. You simply enter the stock's name, the expiration date, and strike price or exercise for the option, and its current price. The program then calculates and displays the days to expiration, theoretical price, hedge ratio, and leverage for the option. *OptionX* will print out this information, and will also calculate and print out a number of other values for each option, including the net premium of this theoretical price compared to the actual price of the option, the brokers commission, expected profit, and return on investment. *OptionX* also figures the volatility of an underlying stock using data retrieved from Dow Jones News/Retrieval. (This option is only available for the stock price data that's been stored on a data disk using the *Dow Jones Market Analyzer* program.)

Comments: *OptionX*, though a well-designed option valuation program, is not simple and should not be used casually by an investor who is unfamiliar with stock options. The instruction manual clearly states that *OptionX* is intended for the user familiar with stock options but unfamiliar with computers, not the reverse.

Figure 12-1. *OptionX*

	Fair	Good	Very Good	Excellent
Ease of Use	☐	☐	☑	☐
Documentation	☐	☐	☐	☑
Reliability	☐	☐	☐	☑
Cost-effectiveness	☐	☐	☐	☑

OptionX is a well-documented program with a good set of screen instructions. The package includes a program disk and an instruction manual. No data disks are required unless the program is used with *Dow Jones Market Analyzer*. The manual includes a detailed description of each menu selection and a discussion of the two option pricing models. It also contains a list of error messages, notes on programming for users familiar with computers, a list of references on the theory of option valuation, and a glossary.

OptionX compares and analyzes the time-differentiated options on a single security so that you can choose the best option investment opportunities on that particular security. One of the parameters which must be supplied to an option valuation model is the current date—the program needs to know this to compute the number of days until expiration. *OptionX* does these calculations automatically, letting you enter the date in any of a variety of formats.

Option prices are available in print from many local newspapers or from *Barron's*. They can also be retrieved from a database (such as Dow Jones or CompuServe) using terminal software. However, *OptionX* has no data retrieval capabilities, so any electronic information must be entered manually. This is certainly one of the limitations of *OptionX*. Another is its lack of graphics.

OptionVue-A

Company: Star Value Software
Computers: CP/M-based computers, IBM PC, IBM PC XT, IBM PC AT, IBM PCjr, IBM PC-compatibles (128K required for PC computers)
Price: $159
Summary: The program computes the expected returns, after commissions, from an option investment. It also tests the results of various option strategies. The call and put calculations use the same parameters, but also use two adaptations of the Black-Scholes option pricing model to calculate the theoretical fair market value of the investment.

You enter today's date, the dividend, ex-dividend date, volatility data, the 90-day T-bill rate, and your margin account interest rate. *OptionVue-A* then calculates and displays its estimate of the option valuation.

Figure 12-2. *Quicktrieve's* **Quickplot**

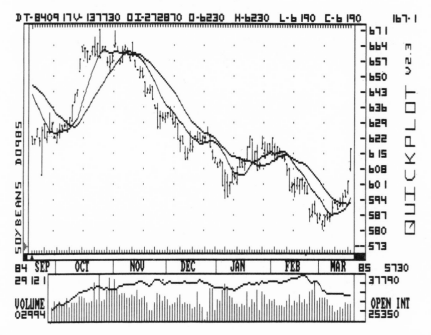

A chart produced by *Quicktrieve* showing the September contract of soybeans.

Quicktrieve

Company: Commodity Systems, Inc.
Computers: Apple II series, Commodore 64, IBM PC, IBM PC XT, IBM PC AT, IBM PC-compatibles
Price: Initial setup is $135 (includes first month connect time), with access charges from $29 per month, depending on data required.
Summary: *Quicktrieve* enables the commodity trader to access historical stock and commodity price, volume, and open interest data by phone or mail-in order to build a personal database. All commodities traded are recorded with few minor exceptions. You can review the data in graphic form with *Quicktrieve*, as shown in figure 12-2.

Yield Calculator

Company: Technical Data
Computers: Apple II series, IBM PC
Price: $275 (Apple), $375 (IBM)
Summary: *Yield Calculator* is a fixed income calculator for determining yields and prices on bonds. You can track a series of bonds and calculate their yield to call date, and yield to maturity. It allows you to try alternative holding periods for each bond and handle "horizon" analysis.

Tax and Financial Planning

Tax and Financial Planning

A *tax-shelter* investment is one which enables the investor to reduce his or her total current income tax liability, delay taxes to a future date, and which provides an opportunity for future profits. Tax shelter investments may prove attractive to executives or to anyone with a variable income, that is, earnings which rise or fall from year to year, as in the brokerage or entertainment industry. Realizing that tax shelters are likely to continue as a major financial service to high income investors, despite pressure in Congress to eliminate such tax-abating investments, several software publishers have created programs for tax shelter analysis.

Tax shelter investment software gives the knowledgeable investor the tools to screen tax shelters quickly. Investment advisors, accountants, registered representatives, and others involved with the individual investor are among those who may also benefit from software which analyzes individual tax returns and the impact of tax shelter investments on tax liabilities.

The software falls into two categories: tax and estate planning or income analysis packages, and tax shelter analysis programs.

Tax and estate planning or income analysis packages enable the user to analyze the impact

Assets and liabilities are key factors in any investor's portfolio.
Courtesy of Lam Der.

of tax advantage strategies on the taxable income of individuals or corporations. Tax shelter analysis programs, on the other hand, aid investors in the evaluation of the proposed tax shelter.

There are two key elements of any tax shelter which must be considered, whether you're looking at a shelter with the help of computer software, or without. The first element is the potential for profit—both in the form of cash flow, and as gain to be recognized on the sale of the underlying asset. The second consideration is whether the reduction of current tax liability offsets the increased risk you're assuming by entering a tax shelter investment. The timing of the cash investment required, together with the extent of your liability, must be factored into any analysis. .

Encore
Company: Ferox Microsystems
Computer: IBM PC, IBM PC XT, IBM PC AT, IBM PC-compatibles
Price: $895
Summary: *Encore* is a financial modeling system for financial and investment analysis; and decision support, planning, and budgeting. *Encore* uses English-language modeling commands rather than the cell coordinates normally found in spreadsheet programs. The program's many functions include built-in U.S. corporate and personal tax tables, accelerated depreciation tables, and regression calculations. It also includes all of the functions normally found in a financial modeling system, such as internal rate of return and net present value. The program's graphics abilities include pie, line, and bar charts, as well as more advanced charts like stacked bar charts. The program also has extensive report-generating capabilities. *Encore* is a procedural language program which provides significant power to the sophisticated investor.

Ex Dividend Stock Monitor
Company: Computer Aided Decisions, Inc.
Computers: Apple II series, IBM PC
Price: $2,000
Summary: The program assists the investor in maximizing total income and total return by monitoring annualized yields, forecasted dividend increases, and ex dividend dates for 150 common and preferred stocks. Program use is based on one

way of increasing the dividend yield of a stock portfolio. Once a stock has gone ex dividend, it's sold and another about to go ex dividend is bought. Once that second stock goes ex dividend, it too is sold and yet another is bought in time to collect *its* dividend. If the commission costs are lower than the dividend payment, the investor has made money.

After entering the required data on the candidate stocks, a yield report is generated. This shows the current yield for each stock and the future yield if the stock was bought and held for five dividend periods, including the expected dividend increase, if any. A quick scan of the future yield column identifies your best income opportunities.

The program is provided with a current list of 70 highest-yielding, liquid stocks which are good candidates for evaluation.

Investment Strategist
Company: Quadram Corporation
Computer: IBM PC, IBM PC XT, IBM PC AT, IBM PCjr, IBM PC-compatibles (all computers require 128K)
Price: $295
Summary: *Investment Strategist* enables a potential investor to determine the economic value of tax sheltered investments. The program calculates four financial measures—internal rate of return, adjusted rate of return, net present value, and net terminal value.

Using these, you can evaluate alternative scenarios and the assumptions of any investment proposal. You can compare the expected return from the tax shelter with the projected return of other investment candidates. It gives you the ability to analyze alternative strategies and do comparative analysis of individual tax returns. More importantly, these analyses are able to project the impact of tax-advantaged strategies to future years.

Financial data for up to 15 years can be entered before the program calculates the economic benefits of the tax shelter. Benefits ranging from cash distributors and capital gains to tax savings are listed. A series of reports can also be printed.

Internal rate of return is derived using the classic equation. The adjusted rate of return is calculated by assuming that all of the investment's benefits are invested at the reinvestment rate, rather than consumed. (The reinvestment rate is traditionally tied to the prevailing risk-free T-bill rate.) The net present value calculations (present value of benefits, present value of contributions, net present value) are computed using traditional time-value-of-money equations. The discount rate is the reinvestment rate supplied by you. Future values are also calculated using the reinvestment rate. They represent the aggregate future benefits that can be derived from the investment. The calculated gross terminal value is the total amount of cash you would have at the end of the investment's life if all the benefits have been reinvested at the specified rate.

The future value of the contribution illustrates the growth of the capital contribution, assuming that it too grows at the reinvestment rate. The net terminal value is simply the difference between the gross terminal value and the future value of the contribution. The higher the net terminal value, the better the investment.

The models created with *Investment Strategist* can also be analyzed using the complementary tax analysis product, *Tax Strategist*, which is described later in this chapter.

Managing Your Money
Company: Micro Education Corporation of America
Computers: Compaq, IBM PC, IBM PC XT, IBM PC AT, Tandy 1200, (all require 128K and color graphics); IBM PCjr, Tandy 1000 (both require 256K)
Price: $200
Summary: While this program is a useful portfolio manager (see Chapter 6), it also serves as a budgeting and tax planning tool. In addition to writing and recording checks, *Managing Your Money* can keep track of your actual expenditures and compare them to your budget estimates in categories you set up. The program contains a reminder pad, a tax estimator, financial calculator, insurance estimator, portfolio manager, and a net worth calculator. Because the components are connected, you can move your budget items from the electronic checkbook register into the tax or net worth estimators.

The tax estimator uses the values from your budget and portfolio sections to figure your tax liability, or you can fill in your own numbers to check possible tax situations. Although the program doesn't generate tax forms, it will print out the transaction details for a Schedule D.

Professional Tax Plan
Company: Aardvark/McGraw Hill
Computers: Apple II series, CP/M-80 computers, IBM PC, MS-DOS computers
Price: $395
Summary: This federal income tax planning tool can provide future projections when you instruct it to apply certain assumptions. For example, it's possible to project tax liability over a time span of up to five years. It's also possible to calculate alternates in preparing for a tax situation in a specific year.

Figure 13-1. *Professional Tax Plan*

	Fair	Good	Very Good	Excellent
Ease of Use	☐	☐	☑	☐
Documentation	☐	☐	☐	☑
Reliability	☐	☐	☑	☐
Cost-effectiveness	☐	☐	☑	☐

Comments: The *Professional Tax Plan* is useful for attorneys, tax consultants, and corporate finance managers. A wide variety of data entry possibilities exist with this program, running from short- and long-term capital gain/loss calculations, partnership income/loss, business income/loss, farm income/ loss, sale of principal residence, investment credit taxes, ten-year averaging, investment interest expense limitations, and cost of living indexing. All are entered as separate data. An investment report is also featured.

An onscreen calculator mode for doing four-function arithmetic during the data entry process is available. After entering data, it's necessary to run a calculation module to manipulate the data and prepare it for reporting. Once the calculation is completed, a matter of a minute to a few minutes, the report can be printed or reviewed on the screen.

If you decide to alter the data to explore other possibilities, you'll have to recalculate the report.

TaxCalc
Company: TaxCalc
Computer: Apple II series, Apple Macintosh, CP/M computers, IBM PC (128K), IBM PC XT, Kaypro series, MS-DOS-compatible computers, Osborne, Tandy 2000, TRS-80 series
Price: $150 (1984 and 1985 packages); $50 for each yearly update
Summary: *TaxCalc* is a tax planning program which can be used with *Lotus 1-2-3, VisiCalc, SuperCalc,* or *Multiplan*. It follows the IRS forms, making it easy to input information. The program does sophisticated tax calculations such as Schedule D, Schedule G, and the alternative minimum tax. It's modifiable and has graphic capabilities when using the *Lotus 1-2-3, SuperCalc 3,* or *VisiCalc IV* spreadsheets.

TaxCalc was specifically designed for professionals such as CPAs, financial planners, attorneys, brokers, corporate executives, bank trust departments, and insurance agents.

TaxCalc's features include:

• Ability to scroll the screen and review an addition to the input without searching for proper category
• Make changes to the input and readily calculate results without moving through the entire system again
• Use of spreadsheet window to watch effect of "what ifs?"
• Utilize graphics when using *1-2-3, SuperCalc 3,* or *VisiCalc IV.*

Tax Decisions
Company: Eagle Software
Computers: Apple II series, IBM PC
Price: $279
Summary: *Tax Decisions* is a tax planning program that enables you to compare alternative tax strategies. *Tax Decisions* is based on the 1040 form and the supporting schedules. The program is easy to run and planning is facilitated through the various options provided. This program should help the investor make the right decisions regarding the tax consequences of investment practices.

Tax Mini-miser
Company: Sunrise Software, Inc.
Computer: Apple II series, IBM PC, IBM PC XT, IBM PC AT, IBM PCjr (128K), IBM PC-compatibles
Price: $295

Summary: This package lets you investigate and compare the tax impact of different income and deduction scheme alternatives. Features like past earning (for income averaging), state tax calculations (optional), and sensitivity analysis add to this program's versatility. Given information regarding sources of income, exemptions, and deductions, the program automatically calculates taxes across a set of alternatives or across a multiyear period.

Figure 13-2. *Tax Mini-miser*

	Fair	Good	Very Good	Excellent
Ease of Use	☐	☐	☐	☑
Documentation	☐	☐	☑	☐
Reliability	☐	☐	☐	☑
Cost-effectiveness	☐	☐	☑	☐

Comments: The value of this package is not that it magically or mysteriously minimizes your taxes, but that it provides you with a tool for analyzing a set of reporting schemes. The tax implications of your options are not always clear—this program lets you identify and exploit all and any potential tax benefit tradeoffs.

Sensitivity analysis further shows the analytical nature of this scenario-oriented package. "What-ifs?" abound, which permits investigation of a myriad of alternatives, instantly calculating the tax ramifications.

A predefined format for income sources and allowable deductions, as well as easy screen editing (such as replicating an item across the set of alternatives), makes *Tax Mini-miser* simple and easy to use. Documentation takes you step-by-step through the construction of a sample case, though once editing and printing commands are understood, new and different applications are easily generated.

It's not clear exactly how the bottom line is, in fact, calculated, since nowhere can the marginal tax structure be entered. Presumably, this is built into the program and limits the longevity of this package to the life of the current tax laws and structure. *Tax Mini-miser* has the approval of Price Waterhouse, who extensively, but not exhaustively, reviewed the performance of the package.

Tax Strategist
Company: Quadram Corporation
Computer: IBM PC, IBM PC XT, IBM PC AT, IBM PCjr, IBM PC-compatibles (all computers require 128K)
Price: $295
Summary: A program for evaluating tax reduction or deferral strategies, capable of computing potential federal income tax liability for up to ten years. *Tax Strategist* calculates the amount of tax shelter you need in order to achieve a desired tax reduction goal. Projected tax calculations are done with several methods, including tax tables, income averaging, and alternative minimum tax. The program can select from alternative strategies for each year and reports may be generated.

   Tax Strategist is useful for the professional tax planner and the sophisticated investor.

ValueWare
Company: David Brown, Inc.
Computer: IBM PC, IBM PC XT, IBM PC AT, IBM PC-compatibles, all MS-DOS-compatible computers (all require 256K)
Price: $250
Summary: A real estate investment analysis program in the form of a template (overlay) for *Lotus 1-2-3*. The manual comes on the disk and can be printed out using *1-2-3*. *ValueWare* can calculate rates of return, cash flows, capitalization rates, and mortgage returns. It's useful for analyzing various candidates for real estate investment and runs quickly through its calculations.

Appendices

Glossary of Financial Terms

advance-decline index
The net result of all advances and declines which have occurred on the New York Stock Exchange or other exchange since a particular starting point. The ratio derived from relating advances to declines provides an overbought/oversold index.

assets
Everything owned—cash, bank deposits, cars, stocks, bonds, investments, land buildings, machinery, furniture, and so on. Property that can be used to repay debts.

bear
One who believes the price of investments will decline. A bear market is a declining market.

beta
A measure of the sensitivity of a stock's price to fluctuations in a particular average. A volatile stock has a high beta, and a low-risk stock generally has a low beta. If a stock tends to move the same as the average, it has a beta of one.

bid price
The highest amount a prospective buyer is willing to bid or pay for a security at a given time.

blue chip
Stock in a company with a reputation for steady growth and profit. The term often refers to one of the 30 Dow Jones Industrial stocks.

bond
A long-term financial obligation from a government, bank, company, or other institution promising to repay a loan, with a specified interest, after a specified period of time.

book value
The net worth of a corporation to common shareholders. Usually expressed on a per-share basis obtained by dividing the corporate net worth by the number of common shares outstanding.

broker
An agent, working on commission, who handles orders between buyers and sellers in a market.

bull
One who believes the price of investments will rise. A bull market is an advancing (rising) market.

call option
An option to buy a specific number (usually 100) shares of a stock at a fixed price for a specified period of time. Call options are often sold by stockholders seeking to increase the return from their shares and purchased by investors hoping for a price increase in the stock (and option premium) prior to the expiration date.

capital
Wealth in the form of money or property. Sometimes the basic sum in an investment enterprise.

capital gain
In the usual sense, refers to an increase in the value of an investment vehicle relative to the purchase price. For income tax purposes, holding period is used to determine whether a capital gain is long term or short term. Long term capital gains receive some preferential tax treatment, while most short term gains are taxed at the same rate as ordinary income. Similar considerations are made for long and short term capital losses.

chart
Graphic representation of selected data. Stock charts usually include prices, volume, moving averages, and price/earnings data.

commission
Fee charged by an agent who handles purchases for the public. Usually a percentage of the purchase.

commodities futures
Contracts to buy and receive, or sell and deliver a commodity, such as pork bellies or wheat, at a future date. The contracts, not the commodities themselves, are bought and sold by investors.

dividend
A proportionate payment distributed to shareholders of a company. For common stocks, the payment can vary with the fortunes of the company.

Dow Jones Industrials
Thirty stocks that are monitored closely. Their collective performance indicates the movement of the market.

efficient market
The theory which holds that stock prices always reflect all available relevant information.

ex-dividend date
The date when the stock sells *ex*, or without the dividend. On or after this date, which is the fourth full business day preceding the record date, the buyer receives the stock *ex* the dividend.

fundamental analysis
The study and evaluation of such basic elements as earnings and dividend growth potential, and the varied impact of economics and politics on the market as a whole or on a particular industry or company.

index
A statistical measurement for comparing a quantity (prices or industrial activity, for example) with the same quantity over some period of time.

indicators
Business-related activities that economists analyze to predict trends.

investment
Any financial instrument purchased in the anticipation of selling that same instrument at a later time for a significantly higher price.

IRA, or individual retirement account
An account established as a form of investment for retirement by an employed person.

lagging indicators
Indicators of economic activity which change direction subsequent to moves in overall economic activity.

leading indicator
Index or economic set of indicators whose changes in basic trend or direction tend to precede and signal cyclical changes in the economy as a whole. Stock prices, for instance, are generally regarded as an indicator which precedes general business cycle changes by about six months. There are also indicators described as *coincident* (change with the business cycle) and *lagging* (change after a shift in the business cycle).

margin buying
Buying properties with money, part of which is borrowed from another party, usually a broker.

market
The place or process by which buyers and sellers meet for the exchange of goods or services for money.

moving average
An average which moves with the unit of time considered. Primarily used as trend indicators, moving averages tend to smooth out short term fluctuations and react slowly, particularly to swift market changes. Often three moving averages are used to indicate short (4–6 week), intermediate (12–16 week), and long (39–42 week) trends.

option
The purchased right to buy or sell at a specified price within a given time, should the holder of the option choose to do so.

portfolio
The total securities held by an institution or private individual.

price to earnings ratio (P/E)
Derived by dividing the price of a share of stock by the companies twelve month earnings per share.

relative strength
The relationship of the price of a stock to the Dow Jones Industrial Average or some other market average. The resulting percentage, multiplied by a factor to bring the plotting closer to the price bars on the chart, shows by the direction of the curve whether the stock is performing better than, worse than, or the same as the market average used.

resistance level
A price area which attracts selling sufficient to keep the price of a stock from rising above it on repeated occasions. Once it has been broken through on the upside, the old resistance area becomes a new support level.

risk
The danger of loss of capital and uncertainty as to the outcome of a course of action faced by an investor.

short sale
Selling shares of a stock you do not own in anticipation of a significant price decline. Shares are borrowed and must be replaced by purchasing the same number at a later date (with the hope that the price will have fallen). This is one method used by sophisticated investors to make money during periods of market decline.

speculation
The assumption of above-average risk in anticipation of commensurately higher return.

Standard & Poor's 500 Composite Stock Price Index
Weighted average of 500 stocks, consisting of 400 industrial, 40 financial, 40 utility, and 20 transportation stocks.

tax shelters
Investments, such as real estate and oil-drilling, designed to defer and reduce taxes.

technical analysis
The study of phenomena internal to a market, such as patterns of price movement, in an attempt to forecast the future movement of the market as a whole or of individual stocks.

timing
Determining the most opportune times to buy and sell securities. Involves identification of both market and individual security trends and taking appropriate action to maximize profit potential. This is one of the most difficult tasks for the average investor, who typically has a record of buying at market peaks and selling at bottoms. A personal computer's ability to handle large amounts of data can make it a valuable ally in the area of timing the market.

trendline
On stock charts, trendlines are formed by connecting the upper points of stock price movement when prices are decreasing and the lower points when prices are rising. The trendline becomes important when the stock price penetrates the line if accompanied by an increase in trading volume.

yield
The return received from an investment or property. The income from a security as a proportion of its current market price.

References

Books
Appel, G. and Hitschler. *Stock Market Trading Systems*. Homewood, Illinois: Dow Jones-Irwin, 1980.

Arnold, Curtis M. *Your Personal Computer Can Make You Rich in Stocks and Comomodities*. W. Palm Beach, Florida: Martin Weiss Publications, 1984.

Bookbinder, A.I. *Computer-Assisted Investment Handbook*. Elmont, New York: Programmed Press, 1983.

Jenks, J.C.. *Stock Selection: Buying and Selling Stocks Using the IBM PC*. New York: Wiley and Sons, 1984.

Krefetz, Gerald. *How to Read and Profit from Financial News*. New York: Ticknor and Fields, 1984

Mick, C.K. and Ball, J. *The Financial Planner's Guide to Using a Personal Computer*. Homewood, Illinois: Dow Jones-Irwin, 1984

Packer, Rod E. *The Investor's Computer Handbook*. Rochelle Park, New Jersey: Hayden Book Co., 1982

Riley, William and Montgomery, Austin. *Guide to Computer Assisted Investment Analysis*. New York: McGraw-Hill Publishing Co., 1983.

Simondi, Tom. *What If? A Guide to Computer Modeling*. Los Angeles: The Book Co., 1984.

Woodwell, Donald. *Automating Your Financial Portfolio—An Investors Guide to Personal Computers*. Homewood, Illinois: Dow Jones-Irwin, 1983.

Newsletters and Magazines
Financial and Economic Newsletter
I.P. Sharp Associates
2 First Canadian Place, Suite 1900
Toronto, Ontario M5X 1E3
Canada
(A free newsletter that describes Sharpe's financial databases)

Wall Street Computer Review   ($39 per year)
150 Broadway
New York, NY 10038
(212) 227-1200

Wall Street Micro Investor   ($30 per year—6 issues)
Wall Street Online Publishing
11 Hanover Square, Suite 1302
New York, NY 10005
(212) 514-5780

Investor User Groups and Associations

American Association of Individual Investors (AAII)
Computerized Investing Magazine   ($24 per year for mem-
612 N. Michigan Ave.   bers—membership fee is
Chicago, IL 60611 $48 annually)
(312) 280-0170

American Association of Microcomputer Investors
AAMI Journal   ($49 per year)
Box 1384
Princeton, NJ 08542
(609) 737-3972

Boston Computer Society
One Center Plaza   ($28 per year)
Boston, MA 02108
(617) 367-8080

Microcomputer Investors Association
902 Anderson Dr.   ($50 per year)
Fredericksburg, VA 22405
(703) 371-5474

National Association of Investors Corporation
1515 E. Eleven Mile
Royal Oak, MI 48067
(313) 543-0612

Addresses
of Software Publishers

Aardvark/McGraw Hill
1020 N. Broadway
Milwaukee, WI 53202
(414) 289-9988

C.D. Anderson
300 Montgomery St.
San Francisco, CA 94104
(800) 822-2222

Altman
Box 1197
Hightstown, NJ 08520

Anidata
7200 Westfield One
Pennsanken, NJ 08110
(609) 663-8123

Apple Computer, Inc.
20525 Mariani Ave.
Cupertino, CA 95014
(408) 996-1010

Avalon Hill Game Company
4517 Harford Rd.
Baltimore, MD 21214
(301) 254-5300

Avinco Corporation
P.O. Box 189
Sharpsburg, MD 21782
(301) 432-4118

Blue Chip Software
6744 Eton Ave.
Canoga Park, CA 91303
(818) 346-0730

The Boston Company, Inc.
One Boston Place
Boston, MA 12106
(617) 722-7960

Brandon Information Management
666 West Germantown Pike
Plymouth Meeting, PA 19462
(215) 828-3249

Bristol Financial Systems, Inc.
23 Bristol Place
Wilton, CT 06897
(203) 834-0040

David Brown, Inc.
Box 10395
Odessa, TX 79767
(915) 362-2008

Bullish Investment Software
P.O. Box 853
Mansfield, TX 76063
(800) 433-3605
(817) 473-9249

Business Computer Network
Box 37
716 College View Dr.
Riverton, WY 82501
(800) 446-6255

Button Down Software
Box 19493
San Diego, CA 92119
(619) 436-2702

Capital Management Systems, Inc.
3800 West 17th Ave.
Denver, CO 80204

Chase Manhattan Corporation
P.O. Box 2985, Grand Central
  Station
New York, NY 10163
(800) 522-7766
(212) 223-7794

Comex
4 World Trade Center
New York, NY 10048
(212) 245-3151
(800) 233-3443

Commodity Communications
  Corporation
420 Eisenhower Lane North
Lombard, IL 60148
(800) 621-2628

Commodity Systems, Inc.
200 W. Palmetto Park Rd.
Boca Raton, FL 33432
(800) 327-0175
(305) 392-8663

CompuServe
5000 Arlington Center Blvd.
P.O. Box 20212
Columbus, OH 43220
(800) 848-8199
(614) 457-0802

Computer Aided Decisions, Inc.
31 Milk St.
Boston, MA 02109
(617) 542-6181

Computer Asset Management
Box 26743
Salt Lake City, Utah 84126
(801) 964-0391

Crawford Data Systems
350 Lantana, Suite 561
Camarillo, CA 93011
(805) 484-4159

DataLab, Inc.
5135 Elkmont Dr.
Rancho Palos Verdes CA 90274
(213) 375-0182

Data Resources, Inc.
24 Hartwell Ave.
Lexington, MA 02173
(617) 861-0165

Davidge Data Systems Corporation
55 Perry St.
New York, NY 10014
(212) 691-4410

Decision Programming Corporation
10401 Grosvenor Place, Suite G-17
Rockville, MD 20852
(301) 493-6444

Dialog Information Services, Inc.
3460 Hillview Ave.
Palo Alto, CA 94304
(800) 227-5510
(415) 858-3796

Diamond Head Software
841 Bishop St., Suite 1618
Honolulu, HI 96813
(808) 537-4972

Disclosure
5161 River Rd.
Bethesda, MD 20816
(800) 638-8076

Dow Jones & Company, Inc.
P.O. Box 300
Princeton, NJ 08540
(800) 257-5114
(609) 452-2000

Dow Jones News/Retrieval
P.O. Box 300
Princeton, NJ 08540
(800) 257-5114
(609) 452-1511

DSF Software
Box 19624
Portland, OR 97219
(503) 244-4800

The Dun & Bradstreet Corporation
187 Danbury Rd.
Wilton, CT 06897
(203) 762-2511

Eagle Software Publishing, Inc.
5350 Cornell Rd.
Cincinnati, OH 45242
(513) 489-7901

Ferox Microsystems
1701 N. Fort Meyer Dr., Suite 611
Arlington, VA 22209
(703) 841-0800

Fidelity Investor Express
82 Devonshire St.
Boston, MA 02109
(800) 343-8722

Flexible Software
134-10 Ivy Dr.
Charlottesville, VA 22901
(804) 979-0973

Galaxy
Dept. LP2
P.O. Box 22072
San Diego, CA 92122
(619) 452-1072

C.R. Hunter and Associates, Inc.
1527 Northwood Dr.
Cincinnati, OH 45237
(513) 761-9322

E.F. Hutton
Contact your local E.F. Hutton
 broker, or call
(800) 334-2477

International Business Machines
P.O. Box 1328
Boca Raton, FL 33421
(800) 447-4700

Independent Investors Forum
1617 19th St. NW #2
Washington, DC 20009
(202) 667-6628

Integrated Equity Planning
98-211 Pali Momi St., Suite 302
Aiea, HI 96701
(808) 488-4766

Interactive Data Corporation
486 Totten Pond Rd.
Waltham, MA 02154
(617) 890-1234

International Algorithms
2318 2nd Ave., Suite 1024
Seattle, WA 98121

Investech, Inc.
P.O. Box 1006
Jackson, Mississippi 39205
(601) 355-1335

Investment Software
P.O. Box 2774
Durango, CO 81301
(303) 563-9543

Investment Technologies, Inc.
167 Main St.
Metuchen, NJ 08840
(201) 404-1200

Investors Software
Box 2750
San Francisco, CA 94126
(415) 981-5261

Investor's Software
Box N
Bradenton Beach, FL 33510
(813) 778-5515 (Nov.–April)
(704) 743-2109 (May–Oct.)

Iris Communications, Inc.
660 Newport Center Dr., Suite 735
Newport Beach, CA 92660
(714) 720-0800

Isys Corporation
289 Great Rd.
Acton, MA 01720
(617) 263-7020

J.C. Productions
8363 La Mesa Blvd., Suite A
La Mesa, CA 92041
(619) 466-5703

K-Wave Financial Services
P.O. Box 1675
Sausalito, CA 94965
(415) 332-9434

Logic Unlimted
7405 University
Des Moines, IA 50311
(515) 274-2541

Matra Communication
1202 Charleston Rd.
Mountain View, CA 94043
(800) 654-0800
(415) 960-3600

MEA Software Association*
Box 2385
Littleton, CO 89161
(303) 796-7100

Mead Data Central
9333 Springboro Pike
Dayton, OH 45401
(800) 227-4908
(513) 865-6800

Micro Education Corporation of
America
285 Riverside Ave.
Westport, CT 06880
(203) 222-1000

Micro Program Designs
5440 Crestline Rd.
Wilmington, DE 19808
(302) 738-3798

Microsoft Corporation
10700 Northrup Way
Bellevue, WA 98004
(206) 828-8080

Miracle Computing
313 Clayton Ct.
Lawrence, KS 66044
(913) 843-5863

Mizerware
A & G Sales and Service
4171 Irving Circle North
Lake Elmo, MN 55042
(612) 770-1373

National Computer Network
1929 N. Harlem Ave.
Chicago, IL 60635
(312) 622-6666

NewsNet
945 Haverford Rd.
Bryn Mawr, PA 19010
(800) 345-1301
(215) 527-8030

Nibble Microspark
45 Winthrop St.
Concord, MA 01742
(617) 371-1660

North American Investment
Corporation
800 Connecticut Blvd.
East Hartford, CT 06108
(800) 243-4322

N-Squared Computing
5318 Forest Ridge Rd.
Silverton, OR 97381
(503) 873-5906

Options-80
Box 471
Concord, MA 01742
(617) 369-1589

PBL Corporation
P.O. Box 559
320 Manitoba
Wayzata, MN 55391
(612) 473-8998

PC Quote, Inc.
401 South La Salle St.
Chicago, IL 60605
(800) 225-5657

Pacific Data Systems Corporation
6090 Sepulveda Boulevard,
Suite 480
Culver City, CA 90230
(213) 559-8713

Pardo Corporation
515 N. Sheridan Rd.
Evanston, IL 60202
(312) 866-9342

PCubed, Inc.
949 Parklane Center
Wichita, KS 67218
(800) 682-2900

Personal Equity Management
System
P.O. Box 2105
Ocean, NJ 07712
800 431-6082

Programmed Press
2301 Baylis Ave.
Elmont, NY 11003
(516) 775-0933

Quadram Corporation
4355 International Blvd.
Norcross, GA 30093
(404) 564-1975

Quotron Systems, Inc.
5454 Beethoven St.
Los Angeles, CA 90066
(800) 624-9522
(213) 827-4600

RLJ Software Applications
306 N. Wolcott St.
Hillsdale, MI 49424
(517) 439-9605

Reveal Software, Inc.
380 N. Broadway
Jericho, NY 11753
(516) 935-2000

Savant Corporation
P.O. Box 440278
Houston, TX 77244
(713) 556-8363
(800) 231-9900

Charles Schwab and Co., Inc.
101 Montgomery St.
San Francisco, CA 94104
(800) 648-5300
(415) 627-7000

SEC Online, Inc.
200 East 23rd St.
New York, NY 10010
(212) 686-2650

Securities Data Access, Inc.
314 West 53rd St.
New York, NY 10019
(212) 621-9097

Sensible Software, Inc.
210 S. Woodward, Suite 229
Birmingham MI 48011
(313) 258-5566

Smith Micro Software
P.O. Box 7137
Huntington Beach, CA 92615
(714) 964-0412

Software Options, Inc.
19 Rector St.
New York, NY 10006
(212) 785-8285

Software Publishing Company
1901 Landings Dr.
Mountain View, CA 94043
(415) 962-8910

The Source Telecomputing
Corporation
1616 Anderson Rd.
McLean, VA 22102
(800) 336-3366
(703) 821-6666

Standard & Poor's Corporation
25 Broadway
New York, NY 10004
(800) 852-5200

Star Value Software
12218 Scribe Dr.
Austin, TX 78759
(512) 837-5498

Statistical Consulting Services
517 East Lodge Dr.
Tempe, AZ 85283
(602) 838-7784

Stockware Systems
P.O. Box 162616
Sacramento, CA 94816

Summa Technologies, Inc.
P.O. Box 2046
Beaverton, OR 97075
(503) 644-3212

Sunrise Software, Inc.
36 Palm Ct.
Menlo Park, CA 94025
(415) 441-2351

TaxCalc
4210 W. Vickery
Fort Worth, TX 76107
(817) 738-3122

T.B.S.P., Inc.
8821 Alcott St.
Los Angeles, CA 90035
(213) 275-0208

The Technical Analysis Group
P.O. Box 15951
New Orleans, LA 70175
(800) 535-7990
(504) 905-1474

Technical Data Corporation
Financial Software Division
330 Congress St.
Boston, MA 02110
(800) 343-7745
(617) 482-3341

Telescan, Inc.
11011 Richmond Ave.
Houston, TX 77042
(800) 752-7001

Texas Instruments, Inc.
Data Systems Group
P.O. Box 1444
Houston, TX 77001
(713) 895-3000

Time Trend Software
337 Boston Rd.
Billerica, MA 01821
(617) 667-8600

Trade Plus
460 California Ave.
Palo Alto, CA 94306
(800) 062-9900

Max Ule & Company, Inc.
202 East 39th St.
New York, NY 10016
(800) 223-6642

Unified Management Corporation
20 N. Meridian St.
Indianapolis, IN 46204
(800) 862-7283

Value Line, Inc.
711 Third Ave.
New York, NY 10017
(212) 687-3965

Vickers Stock Research
Corporation
226 New York Ave.
Huntington, NY 11743
(516) 423-7710
(800) 645-5043

VU/TEXT Information Services,
Inc.
1211 Chestnut St.
Box 86558
Philadelphia, PA 19107
(800) 258-8080

Wadsworth Software
Statler Office Bldg., Suite 1435
20 Park Plaza
Boston, MA 02116
(617) 423-0420

Warner Computer Systems
605 Third Ave.
New York, NY 10158
(800) 626-4634
(212) 986-1919

XOR Corporation
5421 Opportunity Ct.
Minnetonka, MN 55343
(612) 938-0005

Index

If you've enjoyed the articles in this book, you'll find the same style and quality in every monthly issue of **COMPUTE!** Magazine. Use this form to order your subscription to **COMPUTE!**.

For Fastest Service
Call Our **Toll-Free** US Order Line
800-334-0868
In NC call 919-275-9809

COMPUTE!
P.O. Box 5058
Greensboro, NC 27403

My computer is:
☐ Commodore 64 ☐ TI-99/4A ☐ Timex/Sinclair ☐ VIC-20 ☐ PET
☐ Radio Shack Color Computer ☐ Apple ☐ Atari ☐ Other _____
☐ Don't yet have one...

☐ $24 One Year US Subscription
☐ $45 Two Year US Subscription
☐ $65 Three Year US Subscription
Subscription rates outside the US:
☐ $30 Canada and Foreign Surface Mail
☐ $65 Foreign Air Delivery

Name _____

Address _____

City _____ State _____ Zip _____

Country _____

Payment must be in US funds drawn on a US bank, international money order, or charge card.
☐ Payment Enclosed   ☐ Visa
☐ MasterCard   ☐ American Express

Acct. No. _____ Expires _____ / _____
(Required)

Your subscription will begin with the next available issue. Please allow 4–6 weeks for delivery of first issue. Subscription prices subject to change at any time.

COMPUTE! Books

Ask your retailer for these **COMPUTE! Books** or order directly from **COMPUTE!**.

Call toll free (in US) **800-334-0868** (in NC 919-275-9809) or write COMPUTE! Books, P.O. Box 5058, Greensboro, NC 27403.

Quantity	Title	Price*	Total
_____	Machine Language for Beginners (11-6)	**$14.95**	_____
_____	The Second Book of Machine Language (53-1)	**$14.95**	_____
_____	COMPUTE!'s Guide to Adventure Games (67-1)	**$12.95**	_____
_____	Computing Together: A Parents & Teachers Guide to Computing with Young Children (51-5)	**$12.95**	_____
_____	Personal Telecomputing (47-7)	**$12.95**	_____
_____	BASIC Programs for Small Computers (38-8)	**$12.95**	_____
_____	Programmer's Reference Guide to the Color Computer (19-1)	**$12.95**	_____
_____	Home Energy Applications (10-8)	**$14.95**	_____
_____	The Home Computer Wars: An Insider's Account of Commodore and Jack Tramiel		
	Hardback (75-2)	**$16.95**	_____
	Paperback (78-7)	**$ 9.95**	_____
_____	The Book of BASIC (61-2)	**$12.95**	_____
_____	Every Kid's First Book of Robots and Computers (05-1)	**$ 4.95†**	_____
_____	The Beginner's Guide to Buying a Personal Computer (22-1)	**$ 3.95†**	_____
_____	The Greatest Games: The 93 Best Computer Games of all Time (95-7)	**$ 9.95**	_____

* Add $2.00 per book for shipping and handling.
† Add $1.00 per book for shipping and handling.
Outside US add $5.00 air mail or $2.00 surface mail.

Shipping & handling: $2.00/book _____
Total payment _____

All orders must be prepaid (check, charge, or money order).
All payments must be in US funds.
NC residents add 4.5% sales tax.
☐ Payment enclosed.
Charge   ☐ Visa   ☐ MasterCard   ☐ American Express

Acct. No. _____ Exp. Date _____
(Required)

Name _____

Address _____

City _____ State _____ Zip _____

*Allow 4–5 weeks for delivery.
Prices and availability subject to change.
Current catalog available upon request.